Systems in Motion
Exploring Complexity through an Interdisciplinary Lens

LEVEL A

Part of a three-level series

Level A (for ages 5 and up)

Level B (for ages 8 and up)

Level C (for ages 13 and up)

by Jennifer Andersen and Anne LaVigne
in collaboration with the Creative Learning Exchange

CREATIVE
LEARNING
Exchange
Making Thinking Visible

Creative Learning Exchange
Acton, Massachusetts
2014

DEDICATION

To Jay Forrester
for his tireless commitment to making the world a better place
through empowering young people to better understand the complexity around
them and make a positive difference in their own and others' lives.

ACKNOWLEDGEMENTS

This book was created through the efforts, encouragement, and
support of many and is the culmination of learning gained from years of
collaboration with more people than we could possibly name. In addition to
being grateful to our loving families and to each and every person who
helped us along the journey, special thanks goes to those directly
involved in the review, editing, and final project completion:

Jan Bramhall   Michael Radzicki
Joanne Egner   George Richardson
Marcy Kenah   Amanda Wait
Bunny Lawton

Funding was made possible through the generosity of Jay Forrester.

Table of Contents

Getting Started

"Every thought tends to connect something with something else, to establish a relation between things. Every thought moves, grows and develops, fulfills a function, solves a problem."

Lev S. Vygotsky, *Thought and Language*

Introduction

This series of seven interdisciplinary lessons with accompanying free, online simulations has explicit connections to curriculum content standards and to critical thinking skills.

Simulations also illustrate how perceived problems or undesirable behavior can arise from the structure of a system itself, as opposed to outside influences. A system with many ups and downs behaves in that manner because it has an inherent tendency to do so. For example, the very nature of a spring is to bounce up and down, not due to some outside force, but because its structure causes it to do so.

Simulations and Lessons

Each simulation creates an open, engaging environment for students to explore guided and self-generated questions, while gaining content knowledge.

Level of the materials

Most simulation contexts have three levels – A, B, and C. These levels correspond, in general, to different ages:

Level A – Ages 5 and up
Level B – Ages 8 and up
Level C – Ages 13 and up

In addition, since the levels share the same underlying context, a teacher may find using different levels appropriate for differentiation of instruction.

Connections to curriculum standards

Although the lesson contexts may initially seem focused on a particular subject area, each of the simulations relates to curriculum standards across multiple contexts. The table (Figure 1) illustrates simulation contexts, available levels, and curricular connections.

Lesson Context	Description	Levels A	B	C	Engineering	Language Arts	Math	Science	Social Studies	Social/ Emotional
Spring	See how a spring (e.g., a Slinky®) moves when changing its structure and environment.	√	√	√	√	√	√	√		
Relationships	Explore relationships on the playground (A) and in literature (B and C)	√	√	√		√	√	√	√	√
Population	Watch animal populations increase up to a limiting carrying capacity.	√	√	√		√	√	√		
Predator/Prey	Investigate a relationship between predator and prey populations, based on a real island ecosystem.	√	√	√		√	√	√		
Predator/Prey/ Food	Take on the role of wildlife manager to see how the availability of food for prey affects the whole system.	√	√	√		√	√	√		
Burnout	Become a peer advisor, helping students find solutions to burnout cycles.		√	√		√	√	√	√	√
Commodities	Write an article as a journalist investigating different farming practices, while learning about commodity cycles.		√	√		√	√	√	√	

FIGURE 1: Simulations and Context Connections

Implementation Guidelines

These are general guidelines for using the simulations with accompanying lessons and handouts. Each lesson includes suggestions for introducing, implementing, debriefing, and assessing a simulation. Teachers are free to adapt the materials for their own use to meet the needs of their students.

Level of guidance

The simulations allow students to work interdependently with a partner, while following prompts on the screen and within the handouts. Depending on individual and class needs, the teacher may need to provide additional whole-class or small group guidance throughout the simulation experience.

Omit some or all of the handouts, based on instructional goals and depending on student age, reading ability, and level of self-direction. One option is to create a flexible, more 'organic' environment for students to explore the simulations, along with alternate methods for students to demonstrate understanding.

Making predictions and comparing results

The use of dynamic simulations opens possibilities for students to make predictions, design simple experiments, and compare actual results to predicted behavior. These tasks are connected to multiple curricular standards and also enhance students' ability to think deeply about what is causing particular results. The handouts guide students through this process, but conversations before and after the simulation can help students practice the critical thinking skill of evaluating interdependent relationships within a dynamic system.

Assessing student learning

Assessment can take place informally through small group/class conversations and formally through simulation handouts, independently completed written assessments, and oral presentations.

Informal assessment: As students work through the simulations, observe the kinds of conversations they have. For example, to what degree are they able to describe cause-and-effect connections among the parts? For this reason, having students work within a group of 2-3 students encourages collaborative decision-making and reflection as they experience simulation results. While 'floating' through the classroom to observe student progress, ask students open-ended questions about discoveries and insights gained.

Formal assessment: The lessons include handouts, assessments, and suggested projects. Although example student responses for some handout questions are included within lesson plans, no official answer keys are provided. Most questions allow for multiple "correct" answers. Some questions seek an opinion, inference, or interpretation, along with evidence. These questions, by their very nature, do not lend themselves to the creation of a discrete set of answers.

Materials and Logistics

Very little, in terms of supplies, preparation, and materials is needed for implementation.

Printing the handouts

Unless otherwise indicated, handouts are formatted for double-sided printing. Some handouts are optional, depending on prior student experience. For example, one lesson includes a handout based on having read a particular book.

Materials

All that's needed are one or more computers with Internet access and the lessons with accompanying handouts. At the time of this printing, the simulations will not work on iPhone or iPad devices unless a separate flash-capable browser app is purchased and installed. They will work on many other portable tablets. *Note*: if only one computer is available, one option is to project the simulation and use it as a whole-class activity/discussion. For each run, ask students to propose settings, run the simulation, and discuss as a class.

Accessing the simulations

All simulations are available online at no cost from The Creative Learning Exchange via the QR code or at:

https://exchange.iseesystems.com/profile/25/52

All Simulations

Time

Each lesson gives a general guideline for completion time, generally three to four 45-minute class periods to introduce, use the simulation, and debrief the experience. The actual time needed to complete any particular simulation will vary based on individual and classroom differences. Feel free to adjust the amount of time, based on instructional goals.

Last word

How easy is this…really? It's just as simple as opening the link to one of the simulations. The handouts can guide students, so they don't miss parts of the simulation content, but students can also gain new insights through a more organic exploration of the simulations. No one right way exists to use these resources. Explore, discover, and enjoy together with your students!

Simulations & Lessons

"The intuitively obvious 'solutions' to social problems are apt to fall into one of several traps set by the character of complex systems."

Jay W. Forrester, *World Dynamics*

Lesson 1 – Level A
Fun with Springs

Overview

Students explore a simple spring simulation to see how springs behave, given different characteristics. Students can change the springiness, the resistance, and the amount of push or pull.

Learning goals

- Represent and interpret data on a line graph.
- Compare/contrast how different types of springs behave.
- Describe how a push or pull of a spring affects its motion and position over time.
- Identify and describe other examples that oscillate in a similar fashion as a spring.

FIGURE 1: Title Screen

Student Challenge

Design a spring that behaves differently than the examples. Tell the story of how the spring's motion changes over time.

LESSON 1 – LEVEL A – AGES 5+

Time
Two 45-minute sessions

Materials

- One computer for every 2–3 students
- Handouts (See pages 18–22)
- Slinky® or other springs and rubber bands of different sizes to use for demonstration *(optional)*

Curricular Connections

- An object's motion can be described by tracing and measuring its position over time.
- The position and motion of objects can be changed by pushing or pulling. The size of the change is related to the strength of the push or pull.
- Math: Representing and interpreting data*

Common Core State Standards

Key system dynamics concepts and insights

- Springs move as they do because of how they are made; they have the potential to oscillate but can be at rest.
- Movement is affected by characteristics of the spring, such as mass and "springiness."

Additional information, based on Level C simulation

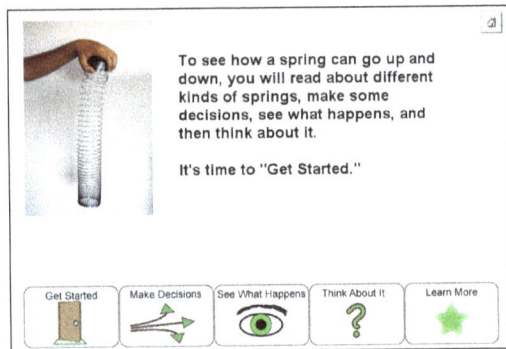

FIGURE 2: Introduction

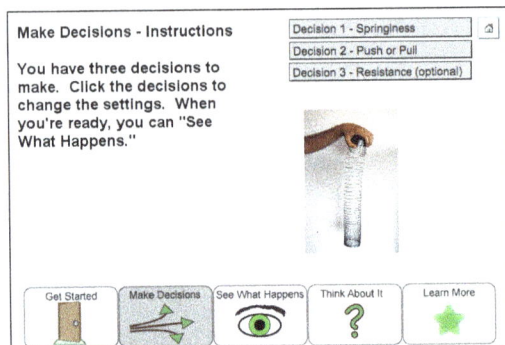

FIGURE 3: Make Decisions

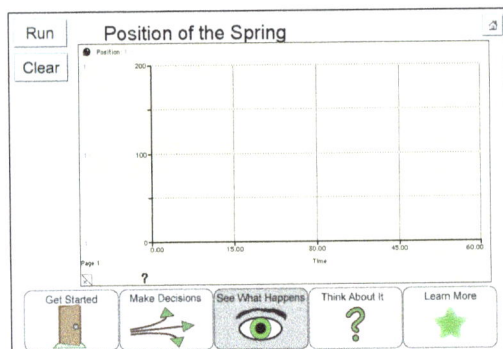

FIGURE 4: See What Happens

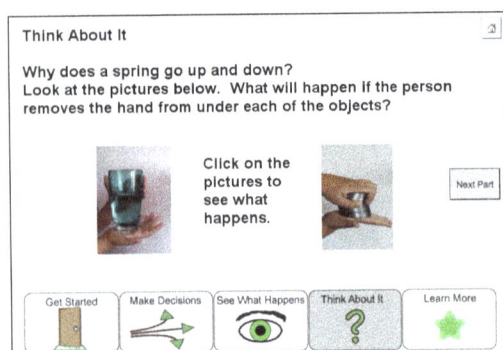

FIGURE 5: Think About It

Lesson Details

Preparation

1. Create groups of 2–3 students each.

2. Copy included handouts for each student group.

3. Check computers to make sure you can access the simulation.

Session 1

1. Introduce students to springs and the key concepts in the simulation. You may also want to have actual springs in the classroom for students to explore (e.g., a Slinky®). These concepts should include:

   a. **Springiness** – How easy is the spring to pull apart? What if it were really hard to pull? Really easy?

   b. **Push or Pull** – How can we move the spring before releasing it? What will happen if we push it up? Pull it down?

   c. **Resistance** – Is there anything that slows down the spring? Does air slow down the spring? What if it were in outer space?

2. Show students the simulation in the classroom and read the introduction together (Figure 2) and go over the "Get Started" section.

3. Using the handouts, have students work in their small groups to "Make Decisions" (Figure 3).

4. Have students continue to "See What Happens," recording data on the handout after the simulation run is complete (Figure 4). Students can run the simulation multiple times for different springs and record their data on the simulation handout for each one.

Session 2

1. If needed, have students complete the simulation within their small groups.

2. After running the simulation multiple times, students can continue to the "Think About It" section (Figure 5). Depending on student age and reading level, students may need guidance with this section.

3. Debrief the simulation experience using ideas for bringing the lesson home and assessment. You can also explore additional models described in the "Learn More" section (Figure 6).

Bringing the Lesson Home

Run some experiments back in the classroom. Ask students to give you settings for a spring that would move in different ways:

- very fast
- very slowly
- very high/low
- start near the floor
- stop moving over time
- never stop moving over time
- others?

Discuss why the spring behaves the way it does for each experiment.

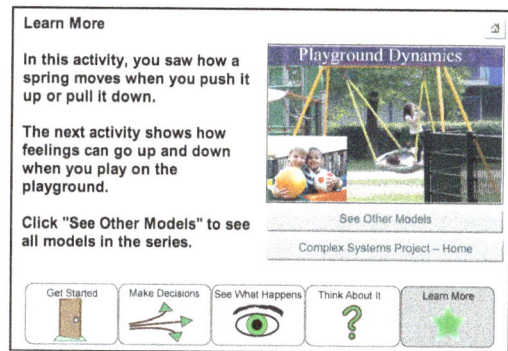

FIGURE 6: Learn More

Assessment Ideas

- Have students complete the assessment section of the handout.
- Have students create a picture of another example of something that oscillates like a spring.

ACKNOWLEDGEMENTS

Lesson 1 – Level A • Fun With Springs
©2014 Creative Learning Exchange
www.clexchange.org

This model with accompanying lesson is one in a series that explores the characteristics of complex systems.

Model created with contributions from Jen Andersen, Anne LaVigne, Michael Radzicki, George Richardson, Lees Stuntz, and with support from Jay Forrester and the Creative Learning Exchange.

Image Credits
Slinky® front screen, boy with slinky, hands holding slinkys, hands holding glass – Images by AML

Kids with ball – National Institutes of Health, Public Domain.

Playground – by Trojanbackoncommons, Wikimedia Commons, Public Domain.

Fun with Springs Simulation

Spring #1

Your spring is very **easy to pull**.

Your spring is **pushed up all the way.**

Your spring is here on Earth, so it has **some resistance.**

What happened? Draw the graph of your spring.

My Spring

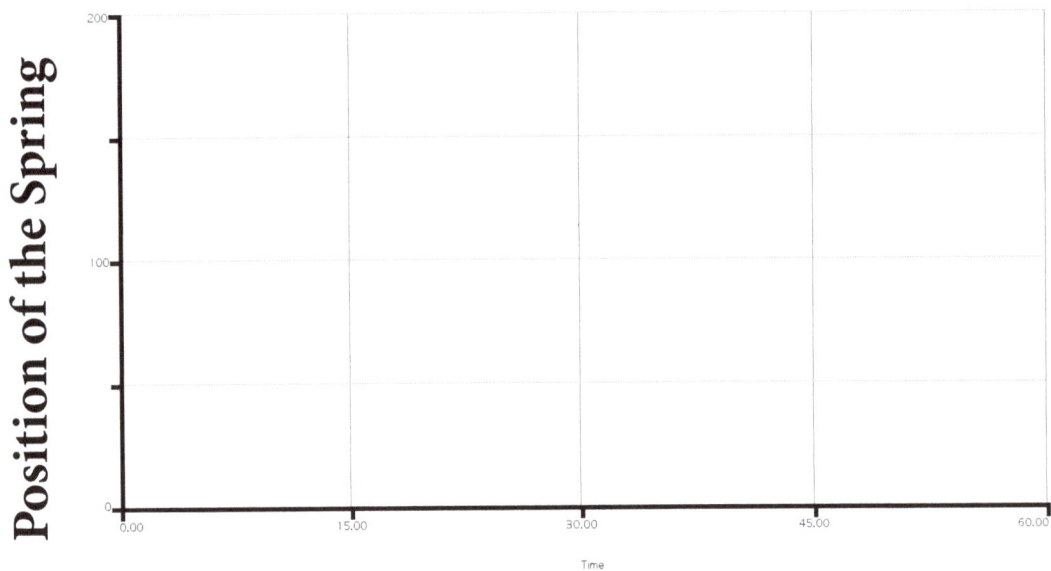

Tell the story of what happened to your spring.

_____

_____

_____

_____

Spring #2

Your spring is very **hard to pull**.

Your spring is **pushed up all the way.**

Your spring is here on Earth, so it has **some resistance.**

What happened? Draw the graph of your spring.

My Spring

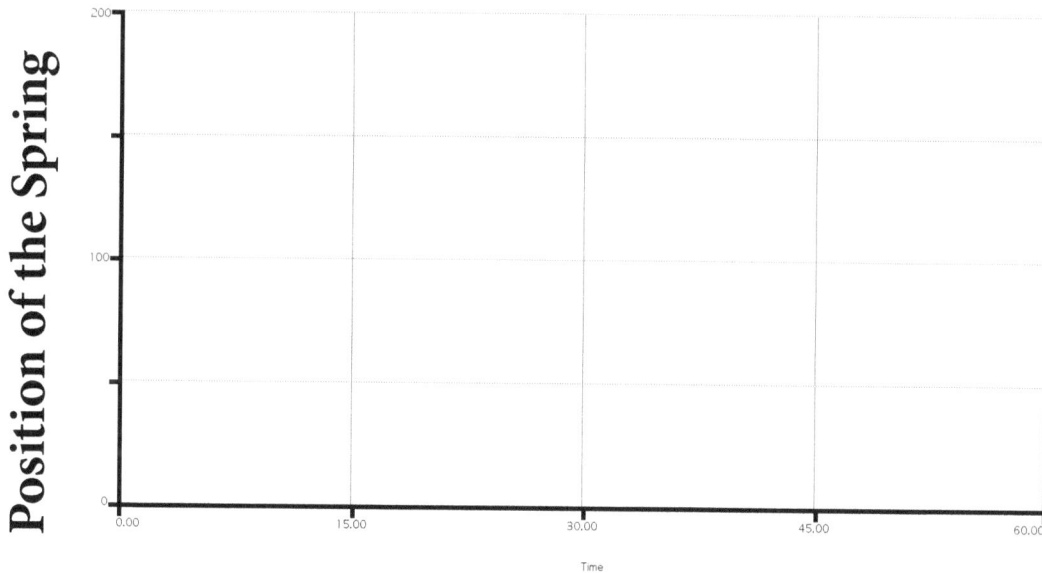

Tell the story of what happened to your spring.

_____

_____

_____

_____

Spring #3 – Design your own spring

Springiness: _____

Push or Pull: _____

Resistance: _____

What happened? Draw the graph of your spring.

My Spring

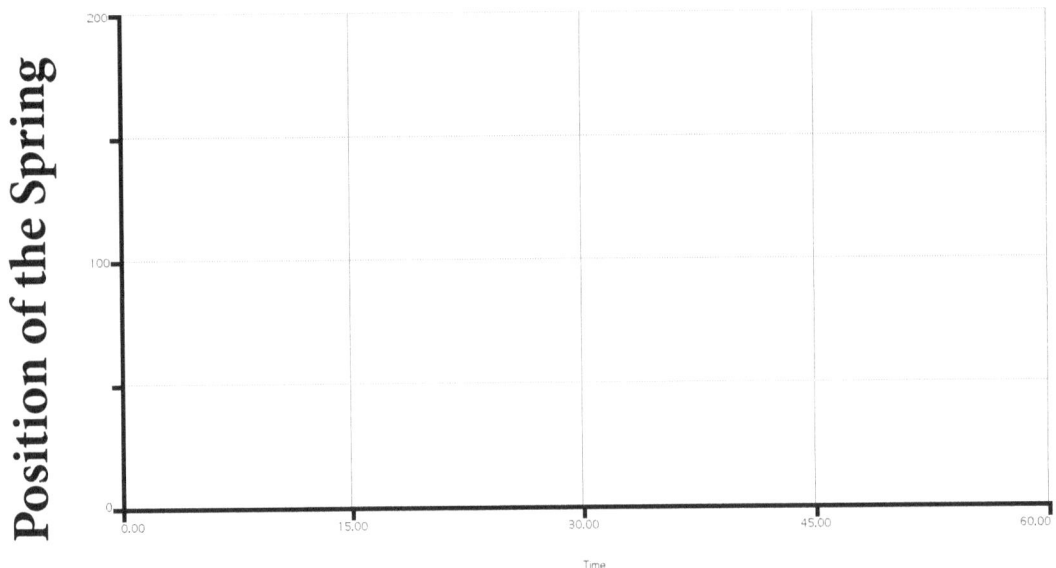

Tell the story of what happened to your spring.

_____

_____

_____

If you have time, you can design more springs. Try to make just one change at a time to see what happens.

Assessment – Comparing Springs
Choose the graphs for two of the springs.
I choose Spring # _____ and Spring # _____.

How are the graphs different?

_____

_____

_____

Why are they different?

_____

_____

_____

How are the graphs similar?

_____

_____

_____

Why?

_____

_____

_____

If you wanted to make a graph like this one, how would you set up your spring?

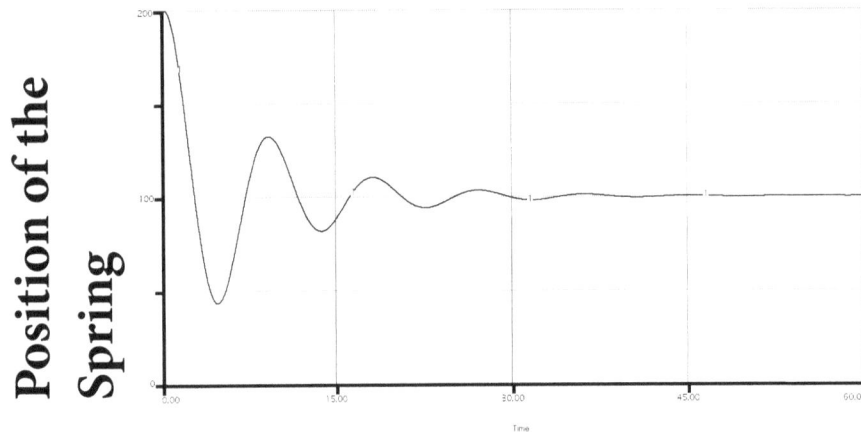

Springiness: _____

Push or Pull: _____

Resistance: _____

What else goes up and down like a spring? Write your ideas and draw some pictures below.

_____

_____

_____

　　　　　©2014 Creative Learning Exchange

Playground Ups and Downs

Overview

Students explore a simulation showing how playing with particular friends might change over time. Students can change elements such as how much they want to play with friends and how quickly they get tired of playing with the same person.

Learning goals

- Represent and interpret data on a line graph.
- Input data to produce a particular pattern of friendship.
- Compare/contrast interactions with different friends.
- Identify and show different types of interactions among friends.
- Tell the story of one friendship loop.

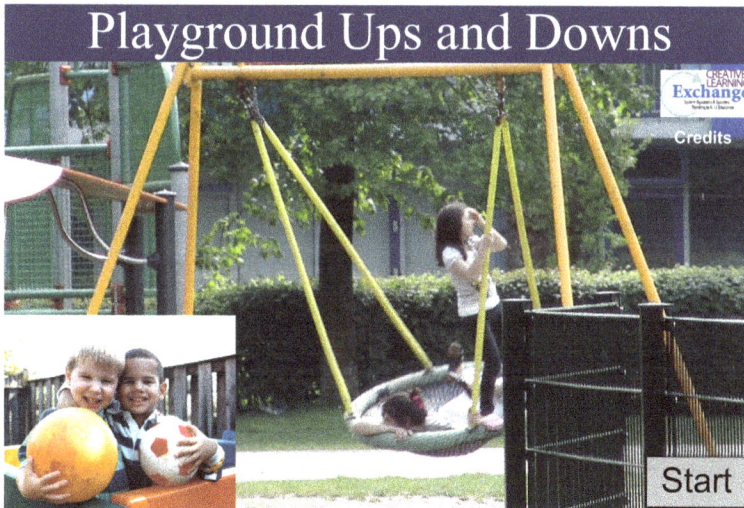

FIGURE 1: Title Screen

Student Challenge

After creating different types of friendship patterns (one that grows, one that declines, and one that goes up and down), assess what contributes to having strong friendships over time and what causes ups and downs.

LESSON 2 – LEVEL A – AGES 5+

Time
Two 45-minute sessions

Materials
- One computer for every 2–3 students
- Handouts (See pages 26–34)

Curricular Connections
- Describe how characters in a story respond to major events and challenges.*
- Write narratives to develop real or imagined experiences or events using effective techniques, well-chosen details, and well-structured event sequences.*

Common Core State Standards

Key system dynamics concepts and insights
- Dynamics between people can seem similar to the movement of a physical object.
- A graph tells a story through its shape.
- Soft variables and ideas, such as love, can be modeled over time.

Additional information, based on Level C simulation

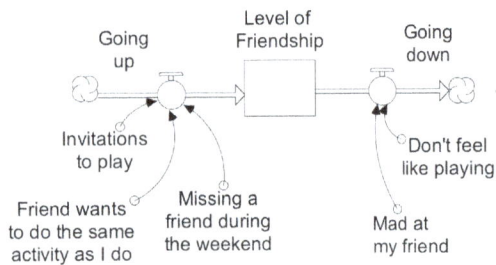

Going up — Level of Friendship — Going down

Invitations to play

Friend wants to do the same activity as I do

Missing a friend during the weekend

Don't feel like playing

Mad at my friend

FIGURE 2: Completed Example

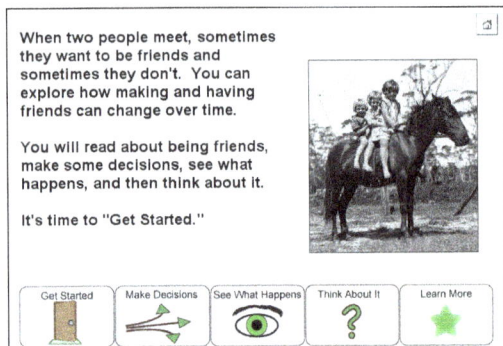

When two people meet, sometimes they want to be friends and sometimes they don't. You can explore how making and having friends can change over time.

You will read about being friends, make some decisions, see what happens, and then think about it.

It's time to "Get Started."

Get Started | Make Decisions | See What Happens | Think About It | Learn More

FIGURE 3: Introduction

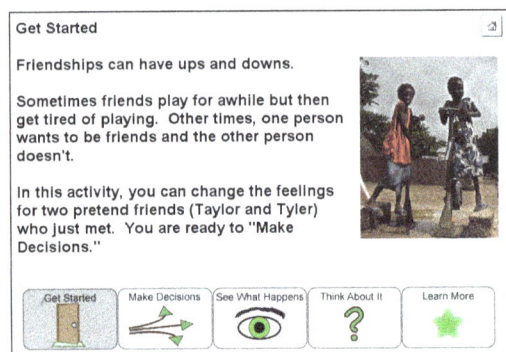

Get Started

Friendships can have ups and downs.

Sometimes friends play for awhile but then get tired of playing. Other times, one person wants to be friends and the other person doesn't.

In this activity, you can change the feelings for two pretend friends (Taylor and Tyler) who just met. You are ready to "Make Decisions."

Get Started | Make Decisions | See What Happens | Think About It | Learn More

FIGURE 4: Get Started

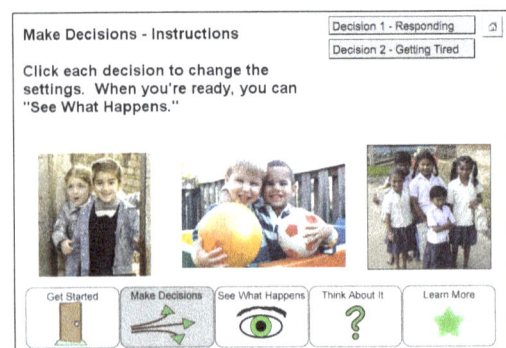

Make Decisions - Instructions

Decision 1 - Responding
Decision 2 - Getting Tired

Click each decision to change the settings. When you're ready, you can "See What Happens."

Get Started | Make Decisions | See What Happens | Think About It | Learn More

FIGURE 5: Make Decisions

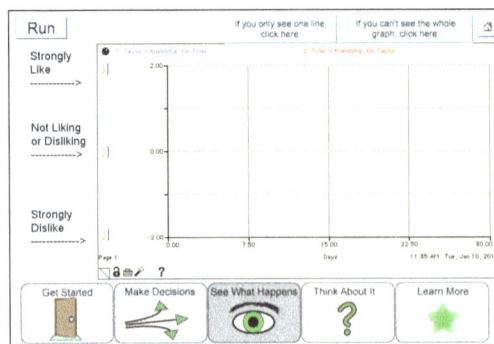

Run

Strongly Like

Not Liking or Disliking

Strongly Dislike

If you only see one line, click here | If you can't see the whole graph, click here

Get Started | Make Decisions | See What Happens | Think About It | Learn More

FIGURE 6: See What Happens

Lesson Details

Preparation

1. Create groups of 2–3 students each.

2. Copy included handout for each student or student group as preferred.

3. Check computers to make sure you can access the simulation.

Session 1

1. Brainstorm ideas about how friends get along or don't get along from day to day and week to week. Why do friends get along? Why don't they get along? *Optional:* As ideas are mentioned, show on the stock/flow template how they add to or take away from wanting to play. (See attached handout on page 26, and example of a completed handout in Figure 2.)

2. *Optional:* Read one or more stories about friendship.

3. Show students the simulation in the classroom, read the introduction together (Figure 3), and go over the "Get Started" section (Figure 4).

4. Using the handout, have students work in their small groups to "Make Decisions" (Figure 5).

5. Have students continue to "See What Happens," recording data on the handout after the simulation run is complete (Figure 6). Students can run the simulation multiple times and record their data on the simulation handout for each one. Note that the graph for each run will always start at a value of 1, showing that two children meet and want to be friends initially.

Session 2

1. If needed, have students complete the simulation within their small groups.

2. After running the simulation multiple times, students can continue to the "Think About It" section (Figure 7). Depending on student age and reading levels, students may need guidance with this section.

3. Debrief the simulation experience using ideas for bringing the lesson home and assessment. You can also explore additional models described in the "Learn More" section (Figure 8).

Bringing the Lesson Home

Run some experiments back in the classroom. Ask students to give you settings for classmates who

- have a lot of ups and downs
- have a strong friendship
- don't get along
- are not friends

Discuss

How are ups and downs with friends in the simulation similar to and different from real situations with friends?

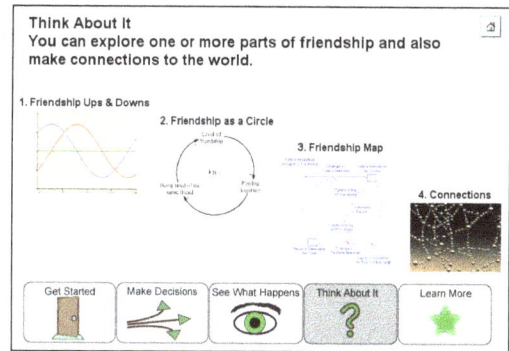

FIGURE 7: Think About It

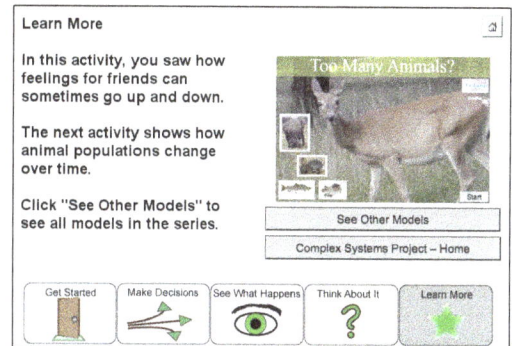

FIGURE 8: Learn More

Assessment Ideas

- Tell the story of the graph over time.

- Complete one or more pages of the assessment section of the handout (pages 32–34).

- Create a picture of friends playing well together. What helps? What hurts?

ACKNOWLEDGEMENTS

Lesson 2 – Level A • Playground Ups and Downs
©2014 Creative Learning Exchange
www.clexchange.org

This model with accompanying lesson is one in a series that explores the characteristics of complex systems.

Model created with contributions from Jen Andersen, Anne LaVigne, Michael Radzicki, George Richardson, Lees Stuntz and with support from Jay Forrester and the Creative Learning Exchange.

Image Credits
Kids on swings, Wikimedia Commons, by Trojanbackoncommons, Public Domain
Kids holding playground balls, Wikimedia Commons, National Institute of Health en: National Eye Institute, Public Domain
Child playing with blocks, painting by Thomas Eakins, Wikimedia Commons, Public Domain
Boy with Bass, Faizul Latif Chowdhury, Wikimedia Commons, Public Domain
Students with tortoise, Executive Office of the President of the United States, Wikimedia Commons, Public Domain

Iraqi Children, US Dept. of Defense, Wikimedia Commons, Public Domain
Kids on horse, Tom Lennon Collection, Wikimedia Commons, Public Domain
Parayar School Children, Jperiapandi, Wikimedia Commons, Public Domain
Senegal children, TSGT Justin D Pyle, USAF, DOD, Wikimedia Commons, Public Domain
Spider Web, U.S. Fish and Wildlife, Public Domain.

Playground Ups and Downs
Classroom Introduction Activity

Brainstorm ideas about how friends get along or don't get along from day-to-day and week-to-week. Why do friends want to play together? Why don't they want to play? Show ideas below.

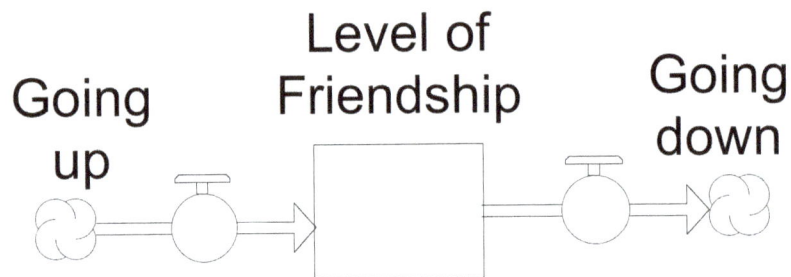

Going up   Level of Friendship   Going down

Simulation

Friend Situation #1 – Set the computer as shown below.
Decision 1: Responding

    Taylor's Reaction   Uninterested o———————● Excited

    Tyler's Reaction   Uninterested o———————● Excited

Decision 2: Getting Tired   Not Tired ●———————o Very Tired

What happened? Draw the graph for each friend.

Taylor: ———

Tyler: – – –

Friendship Graphs

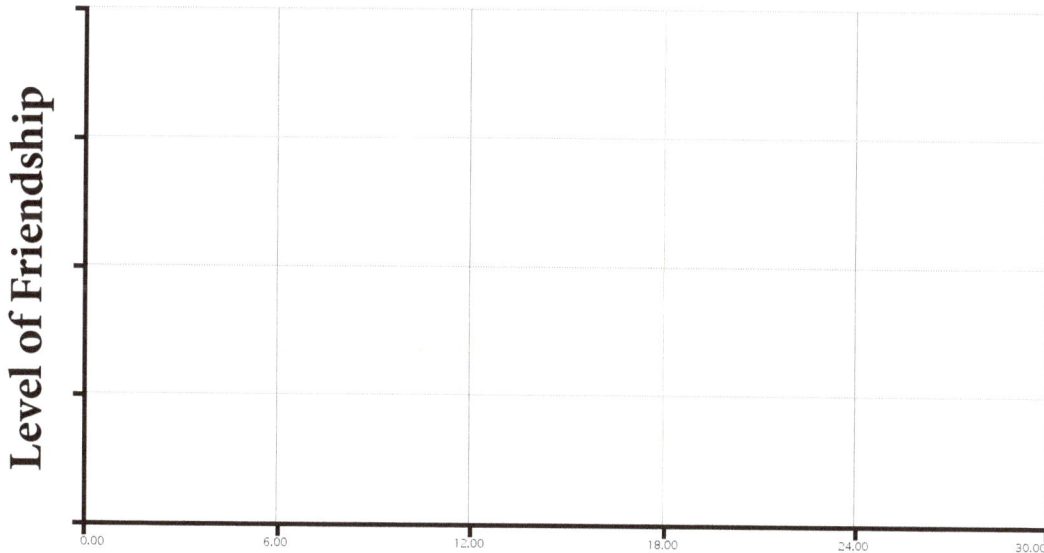

Level of Friendship

0.00   6.00   12.00   18.00   24.00   30.00

Tell the story of what happened to the friendship.

_____

_____

_____

_____

Friend Situation #2 – Set the computer as shown below.

Decision 1: Responding

    Taylor's Reaction   Uninterested ●————○ Excited

    Tyler's Reaction   Uninterested ●————○ Excited

Decision 2: Getting Tired   Not Tired ●————○ Very Tired

What happened? Draw the graph for each friend.

Taylor: ———

Tyler: – – –

Friendship Graphs

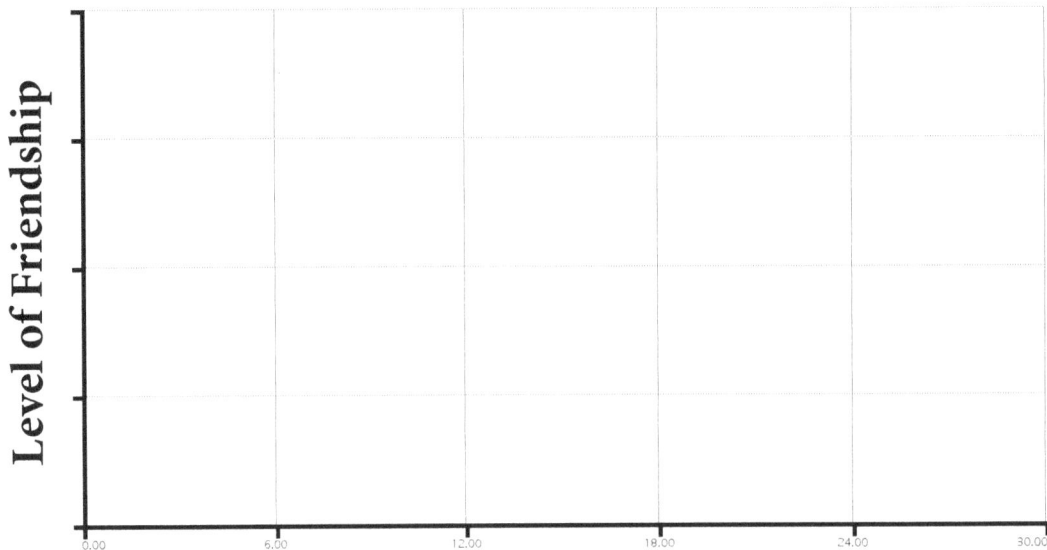

Level of Friendship (y-axis)

x-axis: 0.00, 6.00, 12.00, 18.00, 24.00, 30.00

Tell the story of what happened to the friendship.

_____

_____

_____

Friend Situation #3 – Set the computer as shown below.

Decision 1: Responding

    Taylor's Reaction   Uninterested ○————————●Excited

    Tyler's Reaction   Uninterested ●————————○ Excited

Decision 2: Getting Tired   Not Tired ●————————○ Very Tired

What happened? Draw the graph for each friend.

Taylor: ——

Tyler: – – –

Friendship Graphs

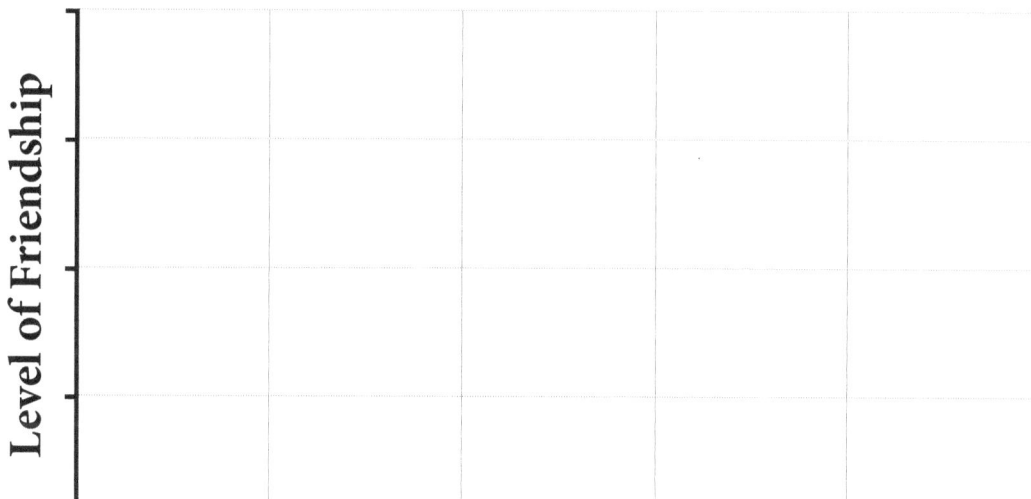

Level of Friendship (vertical axis)

Tell the story of what happened to the friendship.

_____

_____

_____

Friend Situation #4 – Set the computer as shown below.

Decision 1: Responding

Taylor's Reaction   Uninterested ○————————● Excited

Tyler's Reaction   Uninterested ●————————○ Excited

Decision 2: Getting Tired   Not Tired ○————————● Very Tired

What happened? Draw the graph for each friend.

Taylor: ——

Tyler: – – –

Friendship Graphs

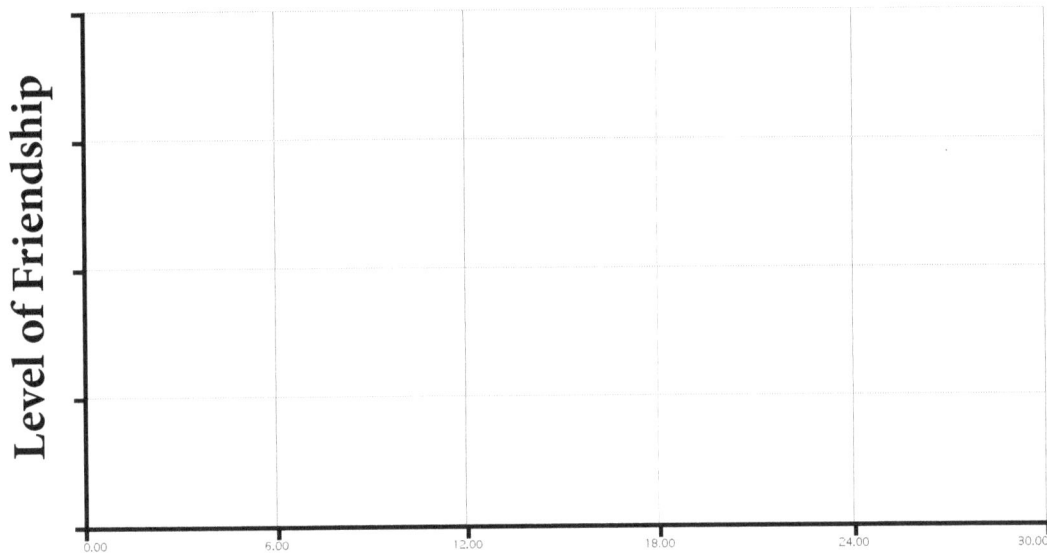

Level of Friendship

0.00   6.00   12.00   18.00   24.00   30.00

Tell the story of what happened to the friendship.

_____

_____

_____

Friend Situation #5 – Create your own situation.

Decision 1: Responding

　Taylor's Reaction　　　Uninterested o———————o Excited

　Tyler's Reaction　　　Uninterested o———————o Excited

Decision 2: Getting Tired　　　Not Tired o———————o Very Tired

What happened? Draw the graph for each friend.

Taylor: ——

Tyler: – – –

Friendship Graphs

Level of Friendship

| 0.00 | 6.00 | 12.00 | 18.00 | 24.00 | 30.00 |

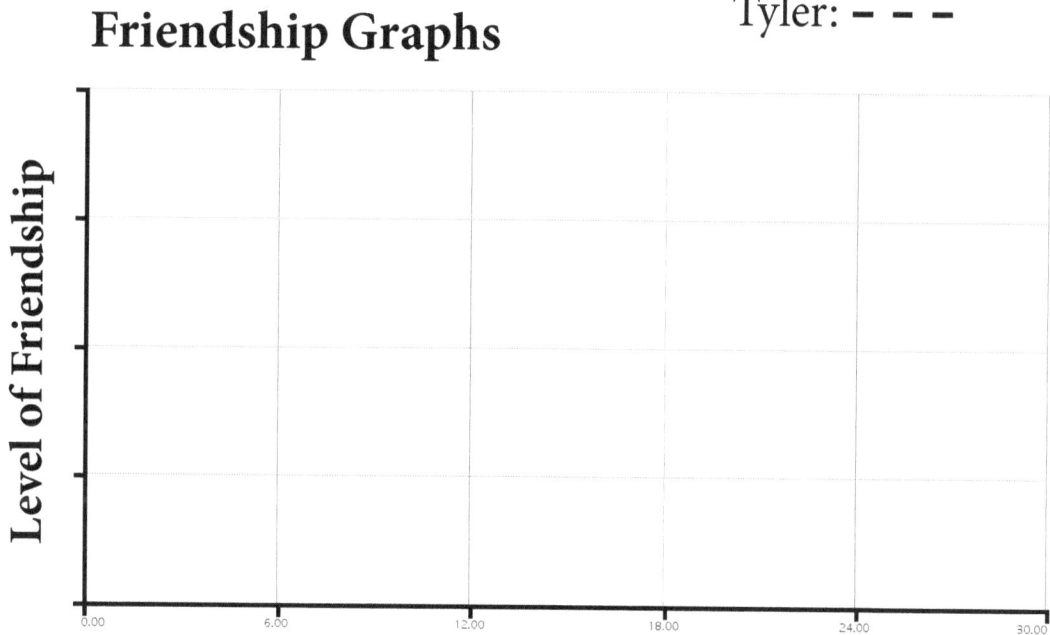

Tell the story of what happened to the friendship.

_____

_____

_____

Assessment – Comparing Friend Situations

Choose the graphs for two sets of friends.
I choose Friend Situation # _____ and # _____.

How are the situations different?

_____

_____

_____

Why?

_____

_____

_____

How are the situations similar?

_____

_____

_____

Why?

_____

_____

_____

Assessment – Best Friends

Draw two pictures below.

When I get along with my friends, it looks like this.

When I'm not getting along with my friends, it looks like this.

Assessment – Story Loop

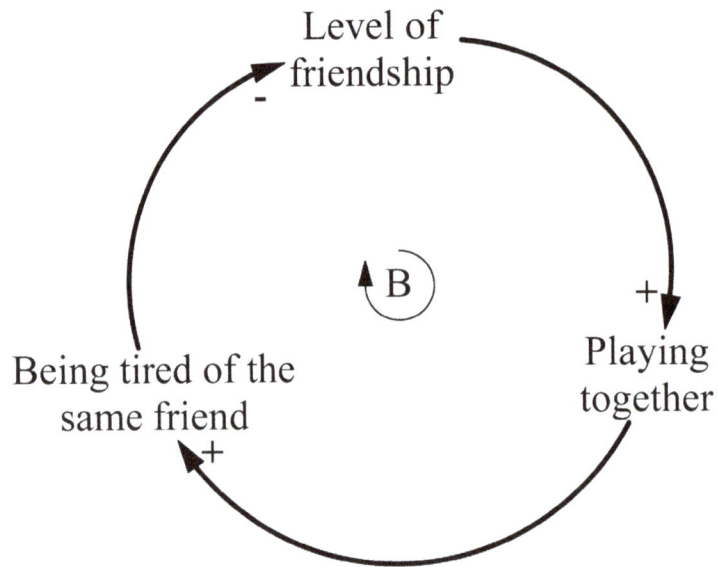

Level of
friendship

B

—

+

Playing
together

Being tired of the
same friend

+

Tell the story of the loop and then draw a picture below that
shows how this works.

_____

_____

_____

Lesson 3 – Level A
Too Many Animals?

Overview

Students see animals all around them, often pets in their home or birds and other wildlife in their neighborhood. This lesson allows students to explore how populations can grow and decline over time. Students can use the information in the simulation (Figure 1) to input settings, such as how long a particular animal lives, on average. An additional option is to have students research, explore, and compare additional populations.

Learning goals

- Explore a population simulation in order to compare animal populations along with how and why they grow and decline.
- Represent and interpret data on a line graph.
- Represent one animal population in a diagram showing how it grows and declines.

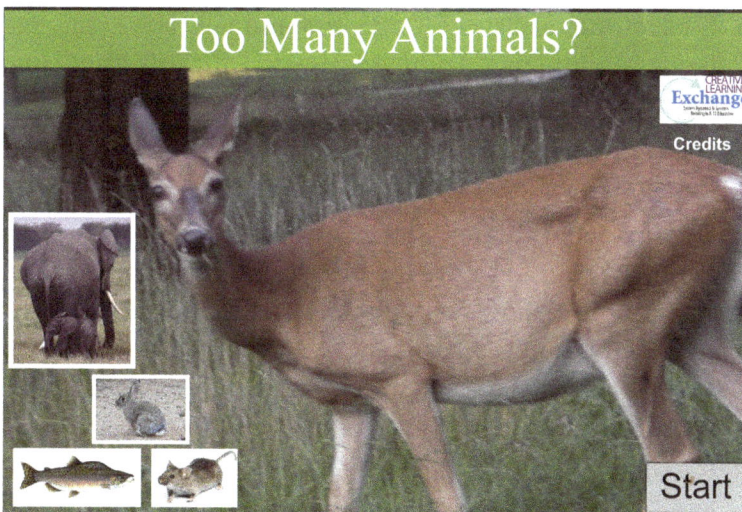

FIGURE 1: Title Screen

Student Challenge

Determine which animal population grows most quickly versus least quickly and be able to explain what created these two results.

LESSON 3 – LEVEL A – AGES 5+

Time
Two 45-minute sessions

Materials
- One computer for every 2–3 students
- Handout (See pages 39–44)

Curricular Connections
- Science: Populations, ecosystems, scientific method
- Math: Representing and interpreting data*
- Reading: Describing connections among ideas*

Common Core State Standards

Key system dynamics concepts and insights
- Nature contains limits (carrying capacity) so that populations do not grow forever.
- Populations may grow or decline to carrying capacity.
- Various factors affect how a population grows.

Additional information, based on Level C simulation

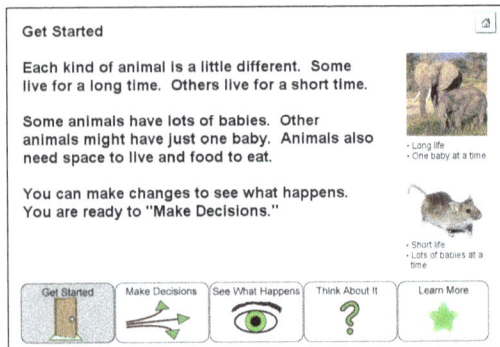

FIGURE 2: Getting Started

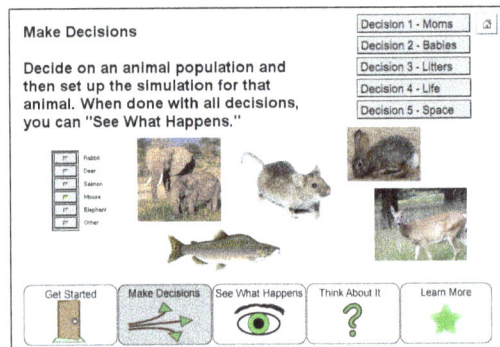

FIGURE 3: Make Decisions

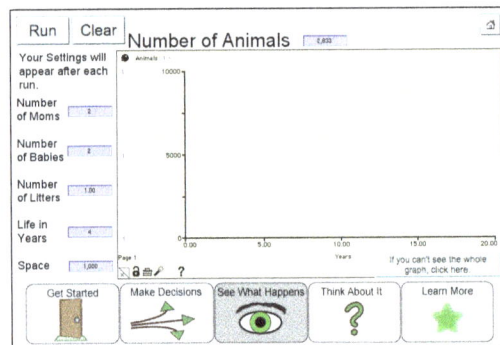

FIGURE 4: See What Happens

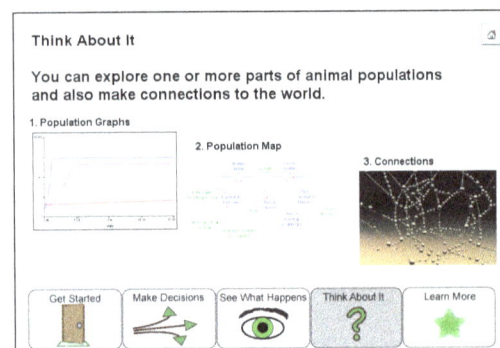

FIGURE 5: Think About It

Lesson Details

Preparation

1. Create groups of 2–3 students each.

2. Copy included handout for each student or student group. Note that you'll need multiple copies of pages 41–42, so students can complete multiple simulation runs.

3. Cut or have students cut out animal fact cards. Note that two versions of the cards are included, one in color and one in black/white. The black/white option is intended for children who are able to read the cards independently.

4. Check computers to make sure you can access the simulation.

Session 1

1. Brainstorm a short list of animals.

2. Briefly discuss:

   a. How long do animals live?

   b. How many babies do animals have?

3. Pass out card sets and have students find matches for each animal on the template.

4. Briefly compare and discuss the different animals in terms of number of babies, number of litters, and lifespan.

5. Look at the card sets for different animals. Have students pick two of them to compare. How are they similar? How are they different from one another?

6. Show students the simulation in the classroom and read the directions together (Figure 2).

7. Guide students to the "Make Decisions" screen (Figure 3). You may want to set up the first animal simulation in the classroom to show students how to set the slidebars for a chosen animal. Initially, have students leave the space set to 1000 units for all animals. They can change this for subsequent runs if desired.

8. Continue to "See What Happens," recording data on the handout after the simulation run is complete (Figure 4).

9. Once they understand how to set up and run the simulation, have students work independently in their small groups to complete multiple runs, recording their data on a copy of the simulation handout.

10. Differentiation idea: Research and run simulations for additional animals and compare the resulting graphs. Note: not all animals will fit within the confines of the simulation parameters. In addition, if sliders are pushed to their extremes, graphs may produce erratic behavior.

Session 2

1. If needed, have students complete the simulation within their small groups.

2. After running the simulation multiple times, students can continue to the "Think About It" section (Figure 5).

3. Debrief the simulation experience using ideas for bringing the lesson home and assessment.

4. If desired, have students explore other available simulations from the "Learn More" section (Figure 6).

Bringing the Lesson Home

- Have students explore the "Think About It" section of the simulation within their small group or as a class.

- Consider why the animal populations did not grow forever.

- Discuss what animals need to survive (food, water, space to live).

- Have students draw one of the needed elements.

- What happens if animals do not have enough of what they need?

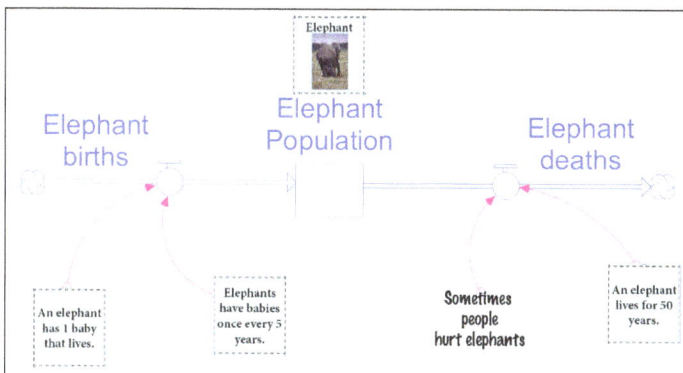

FIGURE 6: Learn More

Assessment Ideas

- Have students choose one of the animals and then use the template (page 44) to draw the chosen animal population in the middle box (the stock).

- Add pictures and/or text (showing babies, litter size, lifespan, space, and other needs) to the template to describe how the population increases and decreases. Younger students can use the same cards from the beginning of the lesson. (See example in Figure 7.)

FIGURE 7: Example Debrief Map

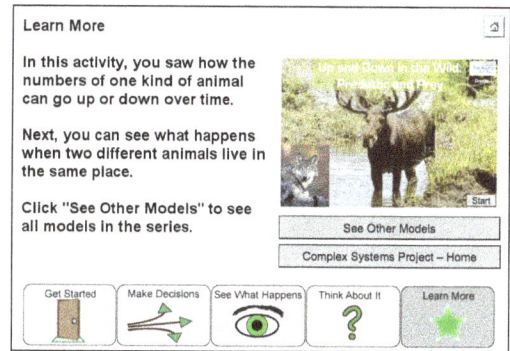

ACKNOWLEDGEMENTS

Lesson 3 - Level A • Too Many Animals?
©2014 Creative Learning Exchange
www.clexchange.org

This model with accompanying lesson is one in a series that explores the characteristics of complex systems.

Model created with contributions from Jen Andersen, Anne LaVigne, Michael Radzicki, George Richardson, Lees Stuntz, and with support from Jay Forrester and the Creative Learning Exchange.

Image Credits
Salmon - US Fish and Wildlife, Public Domain.
Mouse - NIH.gov, Public Domain.
Rabbit - A.LaVigne.
Deer - by Liscobeck, Wikipedia Project, Public Domain.
Elephants - US Fish and Wildlife, Public Domain.
Meadow - Wikimedia Commons, Ace2209, Public Domain.
Elephant with baby - Wikimedia Commons, John Storr, Public Domain.

Baby at play – Painting by Thomas Eakins. Public Domain.
Spider Web – U.S. Fish and Wildlife Service, Public Domain.
boy with toys, Wikimedia Commons, Nationaal Archief/Spaarnestad Photo/W.P. van de Hoef, Public Domain.
Moose and wolf - US Fish and Wildlife Service, Public Domain.

Deer	**A deer has 2 babies that live.**	**Deer have babies 1 time each year.**	**A deer lives for 6 years.**
Elephant	**An elephant has 1 baby that lives.**	**Elephants have babies once every 5 years.**	**An elephant lives for 50 years.**
Mouse	**A mouse has 6 babies that live.**	**Mice have babies 5 times each year.**	**A mouse lives for 2 years.**
Rabbit	**A rabbit has 5 babies that live.**	**Rabbits have babies 4 times each year.**	**A rabbit lives for 4 years.**
Salmon	**A salmon has 5 babies that live.**	**Salmon "have babies" every 4 years.**	**A salmon lives for 4 years.**

Deer	A deer has 2 babies that live.	Deer have babies 1 time each year.	A deer lives for 6 years.
Elephant	An elephant has 1 baby that lives.	Elephants have babies once every 5 years.	An elephant lives for 50 years.
Mouse	A mouse has 6 babies that live.	Mice have babies 5 times each year.	A mouse lives for 2 years.
Rabbit	A rabbit has 5 babies that live.	Rabbits have babies 4 times each year.	A rabbit lives for 4 years.
Salmon	A salmon has 5 babies that live.	Salmon "have babies" every 4 years.	A salmon lives for 4 years.

Too Many Animals Simulation

Animal:_____

How many babies live?_____

How many times each year does the animal have babies?

_____

How long does the animal live? _____

How much space? _____

Write how many animals were left at the end of the simulation.
Draw the graph of animals.

Number of Animals:_____

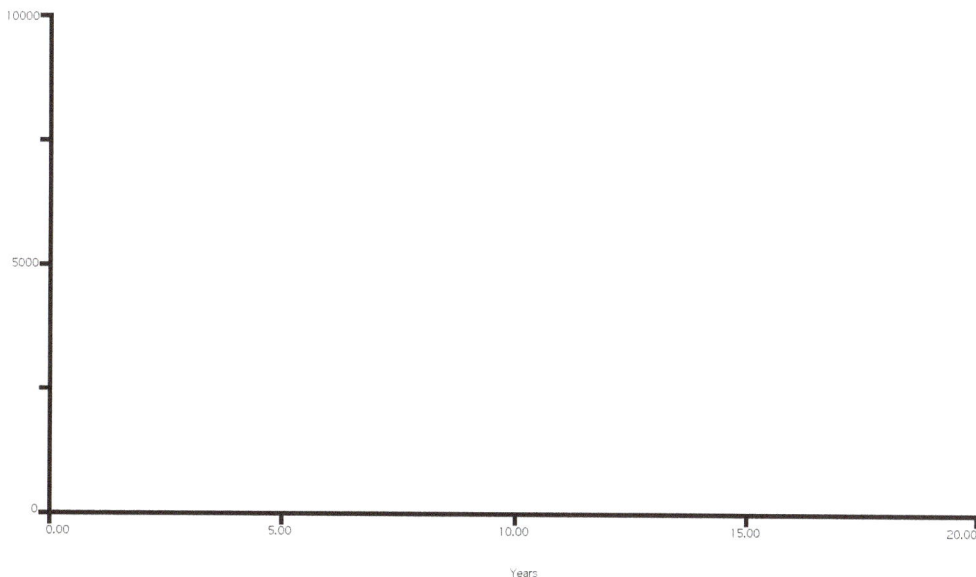

What happened to the animal population over time? Look at the line on the graph to help you tell the story of the graph.

_____

_____

_____

_____

What do you think caused this? Look at your settings for this animal.

_____

_____

_____

_____

Too Many Animals Simulation Summary

Which population had the greatest number of animals at the end?

_____

Which population had the fewest number of animals at the end?

_____

What do you think caused this? Look at your settings for each of the animals.

_____

_____

_____

Why do you think that the animal populations did not increase forever?

_____

_____

_____

Animal Population

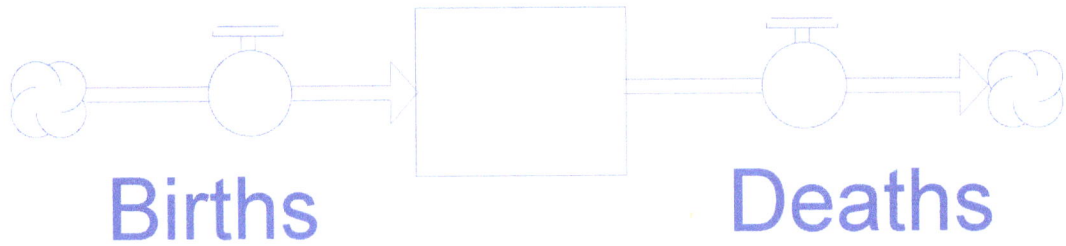

Births

Deaths

Lesson 4 – Level A

Up and Down in the Wild: Predator and Prey

Overview

This lesson allows students to explore the interactions of two animal populations (wolves and moose) within an ecosystem. One animal in the simulation is a predator. The other animal is its prey. Their populations rise and fall (oscillate) over time as they interact and impact one another.

Learning Goals

- Match predators with corresponding prey animals.
- Explore a population simulation with two interacting populations.
- Represent and interpret data on a line graph.
- Tell the story of how and why two populations go up and down (oscillate) over time.
- Identify predator/prey animals in ecosystems.

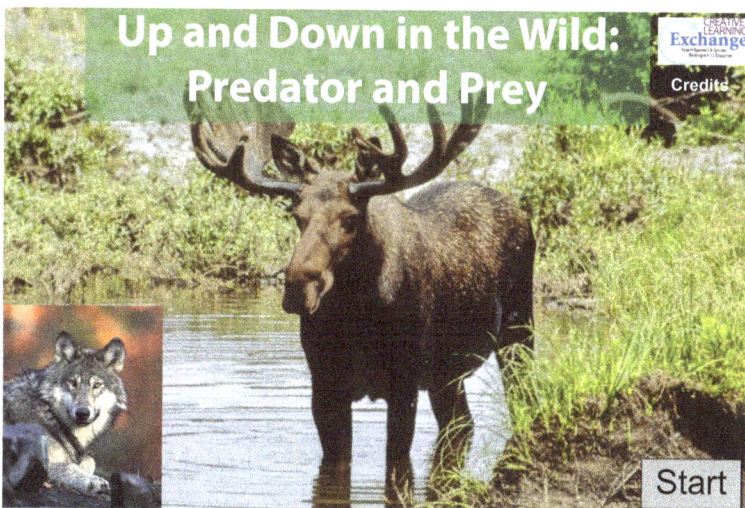

FIGURE 1: Title Screen

Student Challenge

What settings for the moose and wolves create the most stable populations, i.e., with the minimum fluctuation?

LESSON 4 – LEVEL A – AGES 5+

Time
Two or three 45-minute sessions

Materials
- One computer for every 2–3 students
- Handout (See pages 48–53)

Curricular Connections
- Science: Populations, ecosystems, scientific method
- Math: Representing and interpreting data*
- Reading: Describing connections among ideas*

Common Core State Standards

Key system dynamics concepts and insights
- Populations do not exist in isolation; other factors (e.g., number of prey, amount of food supply) affect their growth and decline.
- Predators and their prey form a type of complex system that can exhibit oscillatory behavior.

Additional information, based on Level C simulation

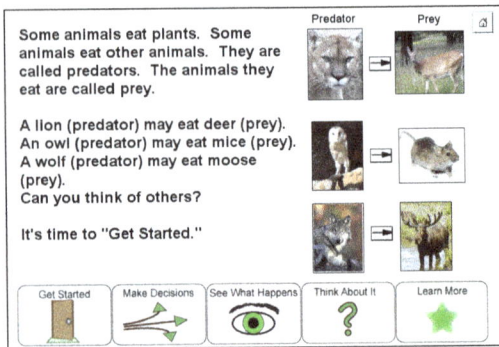

FIGURE 2: Introduction

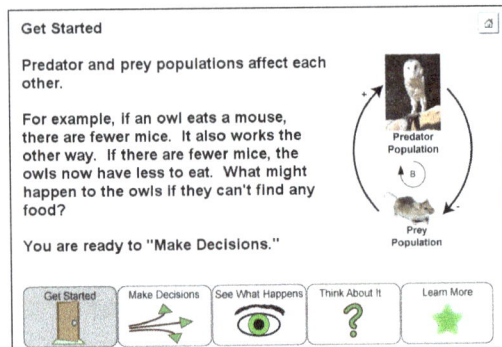

FIGURE 3: Getting Started

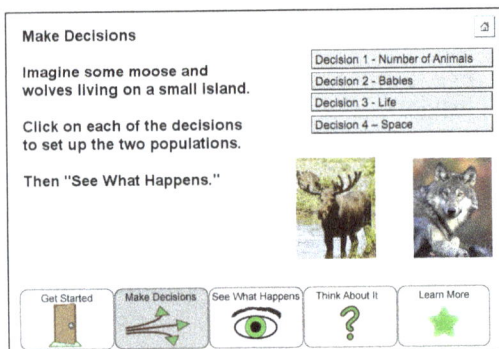

FIGURE 4: Make Decisions

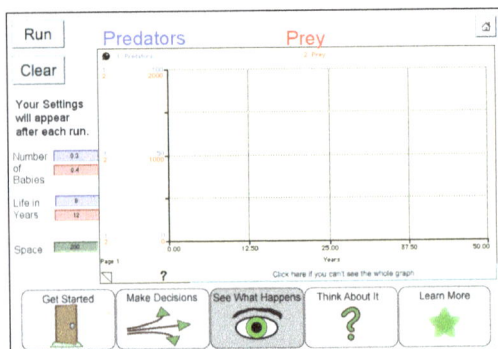

FIGURE 5: See What Happens

Lesson Details

Preparation

1. Create groups of 2–3 students each.

2. Copy included handout for each student or student group. Make multiple copies of the simulation record sheet, depending on how many runs you'd like students to complete.

3. Cut or have students cut out animal predators and prey cards.

4. Check computers to make sure you can access the simulation.

Session 1

1. Introduce vocabulary terms (predator, prey, ecosystem, etc.) as needed.

2. Distribute card sets to student groups and have them find matches for the different predator/prey animals. Students can use the T-chart on page 49 to classify their cards. *Optional:* Provide some blank cards for students who would like to draw additional animals. Students may come up with varying answers. This is one set of answers, based on the initial data used.

Predator	Prey
Wolf	Moose
Bear	Salmon
Coyote	Rabbit
Owl	Mouse
Polar Bear	Seal
Roadrunner	Lizard
Praying Mantis	Cricket
Lion	Deer

3. Briefly compare and discuss the different matches. You may want to note that some predators may have multiple food sources, e.g., a coyote may eat rodents, rabbits, cats, and other small mammals.

4. Show students the simulation in the classroom and read the directions together (Figures 2 and 3).

5. Have students work in their small groups to "Make Decisions" (Figure 4). The simulation is initially set, based on data for wolves and moose on a small island. The moose is the main source of food for the wolves.

6. Have students continue to "See What Happens" (Figure 5), recording their data on the handout. After completing the initial run, students can continue to explore, asking "What if" questions relating to the wolves and moose while using additional copies of the handout.

7. Students can also run the simulation for different animals they have researched and record their data on the simulation record sheet for each one. Note that the simulation results may vary, including some unrealistic results, if they input data that would not make sense. An example would be an insect with a long lifespan and lots of babies.

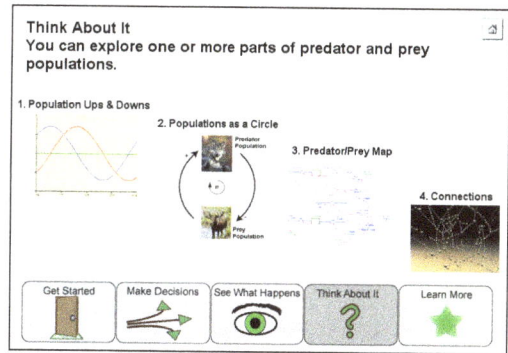

FIGURE 6: Think About It

Session 2 and beyond

1. If needed, have students complete the simulation within their small groups.

2. After running the simulation multiple times, students can continue to the "Think About It" section (Figure 6).

3. Debrief the simulation experience using ideas for bringing the lesson home and assessment.

Bringing the Lesson Home

- Explore the "Think About It" section of the simulation within small groups or as a class.

- Consider and discuss why the animal populations went up and down over time (oscillated).

- Discuss what settings would minimize the oscillations. Test these back in the classroom using a computer/projection system.

Assessment Ideas

Have students complete the assessment handouts to tell the story of the loop, to identify other predator and prey animals, and to share what they learned. You may prefer to have students orally tell the story of the loop. The assessment questions can also be part of a class discussion.

ACKNOWLEDGEMENTS

Lesson 4 – Level A • Up and Down in the Wild: Predator and Prey ©2014 Creative Learning Exchange www.clexchange.org

This model with accompanying lesson is one in a series that explores the characteristics of complex systems.

Model created with contributions from Jen Andersen, Anne LaVigne, Michael Radzicki, George Richardson, Lees Stuntz, and with support from Jay Forrester and the Creative Learning Exchange.

Image Credits
Deer, by Liscobeck, Wikipedia Project, Public Domain.

Lion, Wikimedia Commons, ltshears, 2006. Public Domain.
Moose, US Fish and Wildlife Service, Public Domain.
Mouse, NIH.gov, Public Domain.
Meadow, Wikimedia Commons, Ace2209, Public Domain.
Owl, Wikimedia Commons, Hayleyk, Public Domain.
Wolf, Gary Kramer, US Fish and Wildlife Service, Public Domain.
Boy with toys, Wikimedia Commons, Nationaal Archief/Spaarnestad Photo/ W.P. van de Hoef, Public Domain.
Girl eating, Wikimedia Commons, Renoir, Public Domain.
Hand holding spring, LaVigne, photo used with Permission.

Spider Web, U.S. Fish and Wildlife Service, Public Domain.
Brown Bear, US Fish and Wildlife Service, Public Domain
Coyote, Steve Thompson, US Fish and Wildlife Service, Public Domain.
Lizard, Scott Rheam, US Fish and Wildlife Service, Public Domain.
Cricket (modified version), Wikimedia Commons, Arpingstone, Public Domain.
Roadrunner, Gary Kramer, US Fish and Wildlife Service, Public Domain.
Polar Bear, US Fish and Wildlife Service, Public Domain.
Praying Mantis, Wikimedia Commons, Zakabog, Creative Commons Attribution Share Alike 3.0 Unported.

Deer	Rabbit	Salmon	Mouse
Lion	Coyote	Bear	Owl
Moose	Lizard	Seal	Cricket
Wolf	Roadrunner	Polar Bear	Praying Mantis

Predators	Prey

Predator/Prey Simulation Record Sheet

Predator: _____

Number: _____ Babies: _____ Lifespan: _____

Prey:_____

Number: _____ Babies: _____ Lifespan: _____

How much space?_____

Draw and label the graphs for both animals.

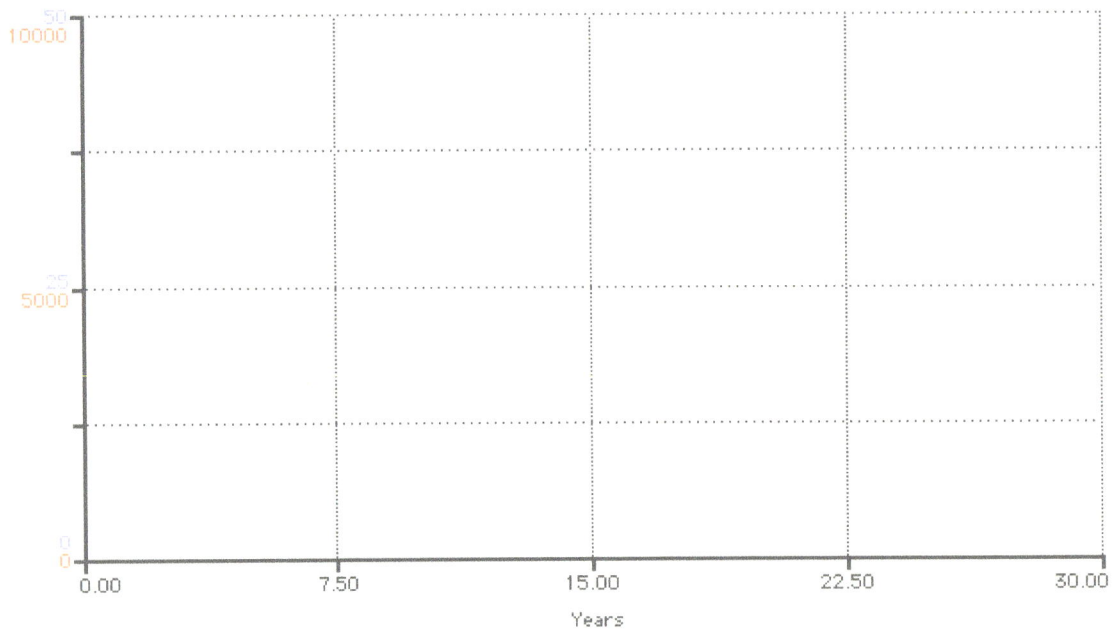

Simulation Questions

Try ideas one at a time and then record what happens on a new sheet.

Question 1: What might happen if the animals had less space to live?

_____

_____

Question 2: What might happen if the animals had more space to live?

_____

_____

Question 3: What might happen if the island had more wolves to start?

_____

_____

Question 4: How could you change the settings so the ups and downs were not so big?

_____

_____

Question 5: What are some other questions you could explore? Write a question below and then try your idea.

_____

_____

Assessment

Tell the story of the predator/prey loop. If the owl population goes up, then...

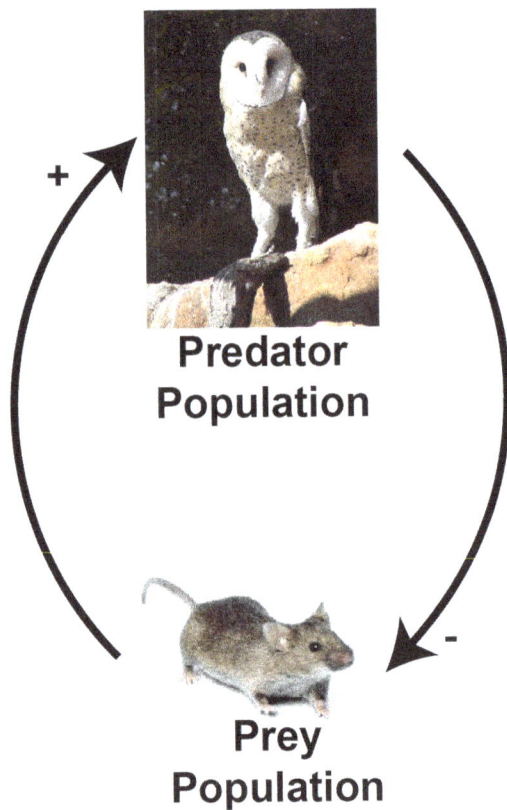

_____

_____

_____

_____

Predator Population

Prey Population

Other Predators:

_____

_____

_____

_____

Other Prey:

_____

_____

_____

_____

Assessment

What have you learned about predators and their prey?

_____

_____

_____

_____

Why do populations go up and down?

_____

_____

_____

_____

What did you change to keep the populations from going up and down as much?

_____

_____

_____

_____

Lesson 5 – Level A
All Together Now: Predator, Prey, and Plants

Overview

This lesson allows students to explore the interactions of two animal populations (wolves and moose) and plants within an ecosystem. The populations and the plants rise and fall (oscillate) over time as they interact and impact one another.

Learning Goals

- Match predators with corresponding prey animals.
- Match prey with corresponding food sources.
- Explore a population simulation with two interacting populations and a food source.
- Represent and interpret data on a line graph.
- Tell the story of how and why two populations and a food supply go up and down (oscillate) over time.

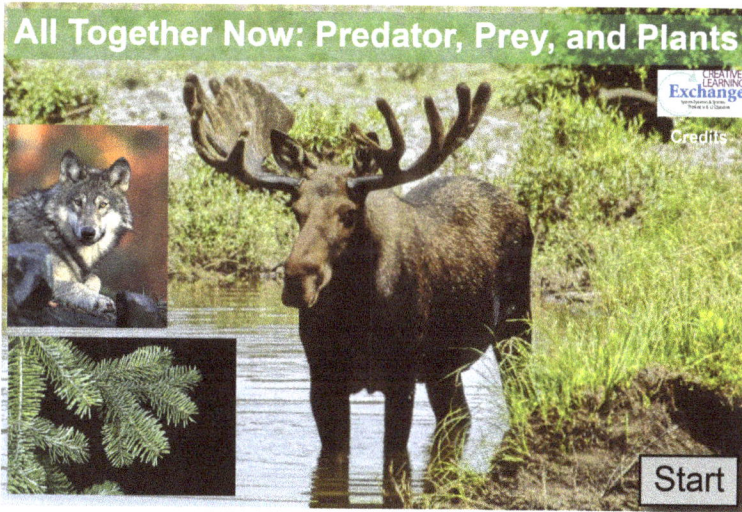

FIGURE 1: Title Screen

Student Challenge

Set up a level of hunting that keeps the populations of predators and prey at healthy levels.

LESSON 5 – LEVEL A – AGES 5+

Time
Two or three 45-minute sessions

Materials
- One computer for every 2–3 students
- Handout (See pages 59–64)

Curricular Connections
- Science: Populations, ecosystems, scientific method
- Math: Representing and interpreting data*
- Reading: Describing connections among ideas*

Common Core State Standards

Key system dynamics concepts and insights
- Populations do not exist in isolation; other factors (e.g., number of prey, amount of food supply) affect their growth and decline.
- Predators, their prey, and food for the prey form a type of complex system that can exhibit oscillatory behavior.

Additional information, based on Level C simulation

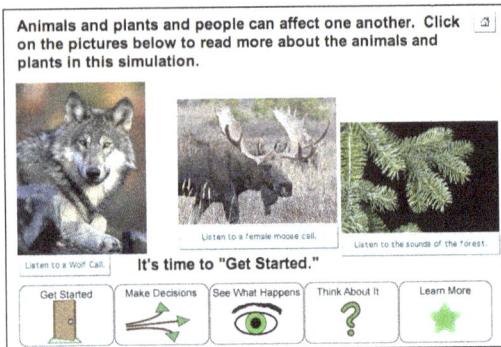

FIGURE 2: Introduction

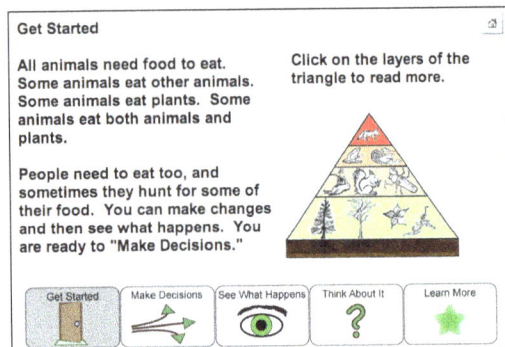

FIGURE 3: Getting Started

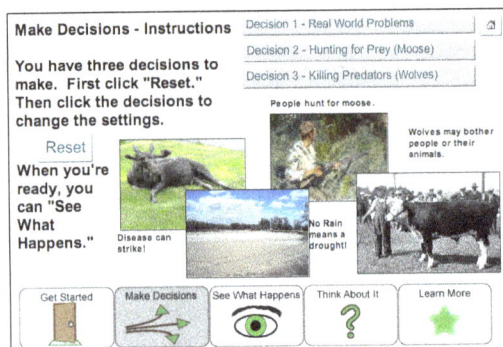

FIGURE 4: Make Decisions

Lesson Details

Preparation

1. Create groups of 2–3 students each.

2. Copy included handout for each student or student group. Make multiple copies of the simulation record sheet, depending on how many runs you'd like students to complete.

3. Cut or have students cut out cards for predators, prey, and food (Handout, page 1).

4. Check computers to make sure you can access the simulation.

Session 1

1. Introduce vocabulary terms (predator, prey, food, ecosystem, etc.) as needed.

2. Distribute card sets to student groups and have them find matches for the different predator/prey animals. Students can use the chart (Handout, page 2) to classify their cards. *Optional:* Provide some blank cards for students who would like to draw additional animals and plants. Students may have varying answers. This is one set of answers. Note that only plant-based food was included in the set of cards. Some prey animals may eat other organisms or may be omnivores. For example, a roadrunner eats lizards and a lizard eat insects.

Predator	Prey	Food
Wolf	Moose	Balsam Fir
Coyote	Rabbit	Grassland
Owl	Mouse	Wild Rice
Lion	Deer	Wetlands

3. Briefly compare and discuss the different matches. You may want to note that some predators have multiple food sources, e.g., a coyote may eat rodents, rabbits, cats, and other small mammals.

4. Show students the simulation in the classroom and read the introduction together (Figures 2 and 3).

5. Have students work in their small groups to "Make Decisions" (Figure 4). The simulation is initially set with no "real-world" problems and no hunting.

6. Have students continue to "See What Happens" (Figure 5), recording their data on Handout, page 3. After completing the initial baseline run, students can continue to explore, asking "What if" questions (Handout, page 4) relating to the wolves, the moose, and the food (plants) while using additional copies of Handout, page 3.

Session 2 and beyond

1. If needed, have students complete the simulation within their small groups.

2. After running the simulation multiple times, students continue to the "Think About It" section (Figure 6).

3. Debrief the simulation experience using ideas for bringing the lesson home and assessment (Handouts, page 5 and page 6).

Bringing the Lesson Home

- Explore the "Think About It" section of the simulation within small groups or as a class.

- Consider why the animal populations and food went up and down (oscillated) over time.

- Discuss issues and test ideas back in the classroom using a computer/ projector. For example:
  - settings that flatten the oscillations.
  - settings that allow for hunting of moose while keeping the ecosystem healthy.
  - settings that keep people and their animals safe.

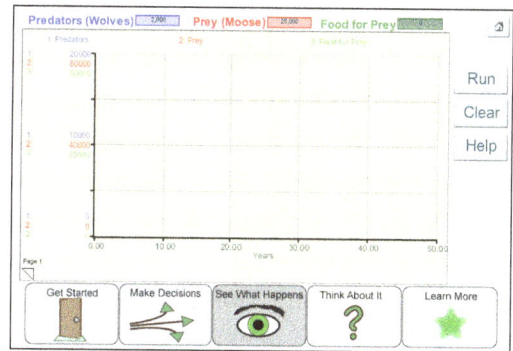

FIGURE 5: See What Happens

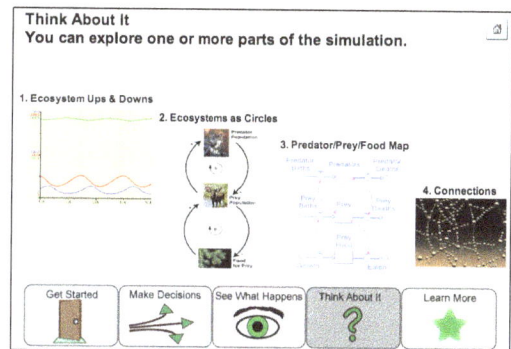

FIGURE 6: Think About It

Assessment Ideas

Have students complete the assessment handouts to tell the story of the loops; to identify other predators, prey, and food; and to share what they learned. You may prefer to have students orally tell the story of the loops. The assessment questions can also be part of a class discussion.

ACKNOWLEDGEMENTS

Lesson 5 – Level A • All Together Now: Predator, Prey, and Plants
©2014 Creative Learning Exchange
www.clexchange.org

This model with accompanying lesson is one in a series that explores the characteristics of complex systems.

Model created with contributions from Jen Andersen, Anne LaVigne, Michael Radzicki, George Richardson, Lees Stuntz, and with support from Jay Forrester and the Creative Learning Exchange.

Image Credits

Wolf, Gary Kramer, USFWS, Public Domain.

Balsam Fir, USDA, Public Domain.

Moose (title page), USFWS, Public Domain.

Moose (intro page), USFWS, Public Domain.

Wolf call, USFWS, Public Domain.

Sound wave, USFWS, Public Domain.

Moose call, USFWS, Public Domain.

Trophic pyramid, by Thompsma, Wikimedia Commons, Creative Commons Attribution -ShareAlike 3.0 Unported license (http://creativecommons.org/licenses/by-sa/3.0/deed.en).

Moose reclining, by Zaereth, Wikimedia Commons, Public Domain.

Hunter painting, Bruno Liljefors, Public Domain.

Boy with cow, ca.1923, Public Domain.

Dry riverbed, Kirk Miller, USGS, US Dept. of the Interior, Public Domain.

Spider web, USFWS, Public Domain.

Spring, Photo by A.LaVigne, Used with Permission.

City scene, Detroit Publishing Company, ca.1900, Public Domain.

Toy stuffed monkey, by Richfife, Wikimedia Commons, Public Domain.

Sounds of the forest, by Dobride, Freesound.org, Creative Commons Attribution License.

Wild Rice, by Chemoqua, Wikimedia Commons, Public Domain

Wetlands, USFWS, Public Domain.

Grassland, by Luke N. Vargas, Wikimedia Commons, Public Domain

Deer	Rabbit	Owl

Lion	Coyote	Grassland

Moose	Mouse	Wetlands

Wolf	Wild Rice	Balsam Fir

Predators	Prey	Food

Predator/Prey/Food Simulation Record Sheet

Real-World Problems: _____

Hunting for Prey (Moose): _____

Killing Predators (Wolves): Yes or No

Draw and label the graphs for both animals and food.

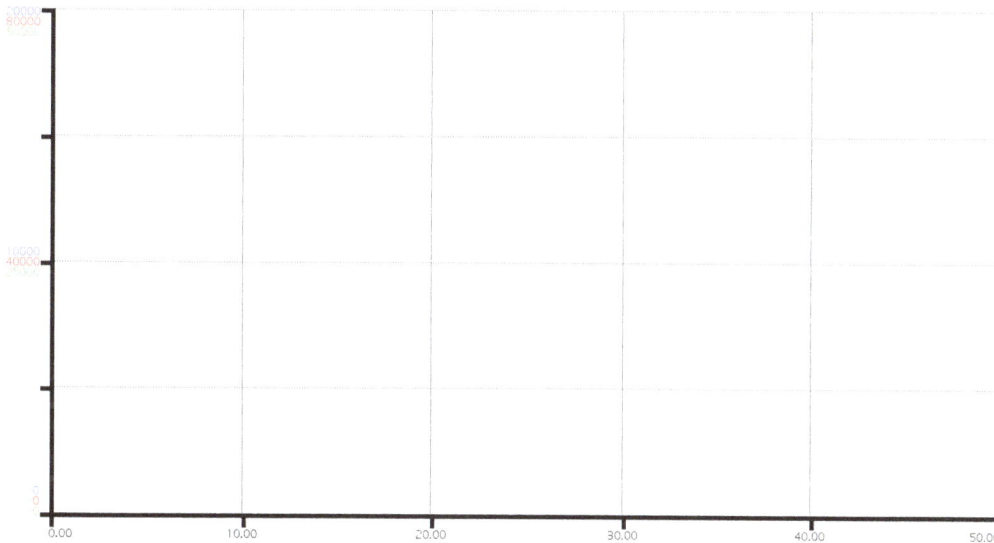

What happened?

_____

_____

_____

Simulation Questions

Try ideas one at a time and then record what happens on a new sheet.

Question 1: What happens if I make no changes?

Question 2: What happens if the moose get a disease?

Question 3: What happens if it doesn't rain, and there's a drought?

Question 4: What happens if people hunt for a lot of moose?

Question 5: What happens if people kill all the wolves?

Question 6: How can people hunt and still have a healthy ecosystem?

Question 7: What are some other questions you could explore? Write a question below and then try your idea.

_____

_____

_____

_____

_____

Assessment 1

Tell the story of the predator/prey/food loops. If the wolf population goes up, then...

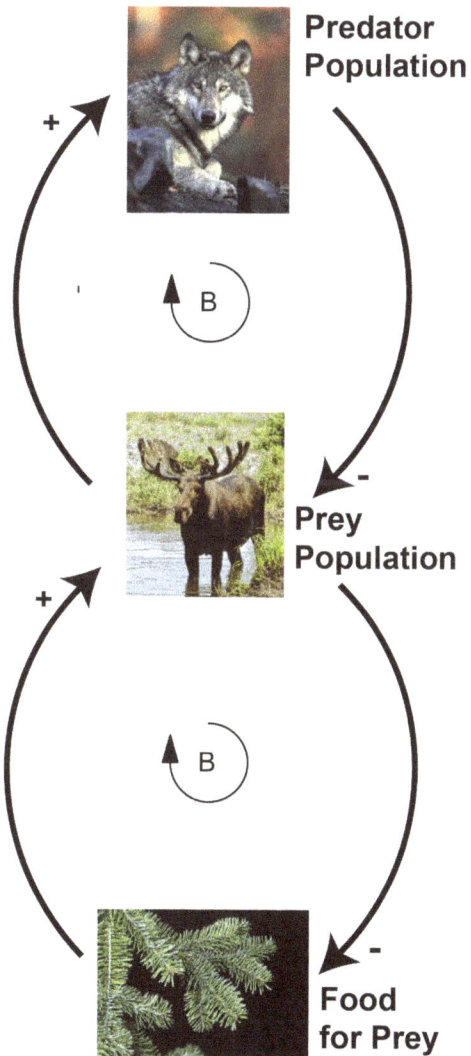

_____

_____

_____

Predator Population

+

B

Prey Population

+

−

B

Food for Prey

−

Other Predators:

_____

_____

_____

_____

Other Prey:

_____

_____

_____

Other Food:

_____

_____

_____

_____

Assessment 2

What have you learned about predators, prey, and food?

_____

_____

_____

_____

_____

Why do populations go up and down?

_____

_____

_____

Why does the food go up and down?

_____

_____

_____

Everything Else

"You can't navigate well in an interconnected, feedback-dominated world unless you take your eyes off short-term events and look for long-term behavior and structure…."

Donella Meadows, *Thinking in Systems*

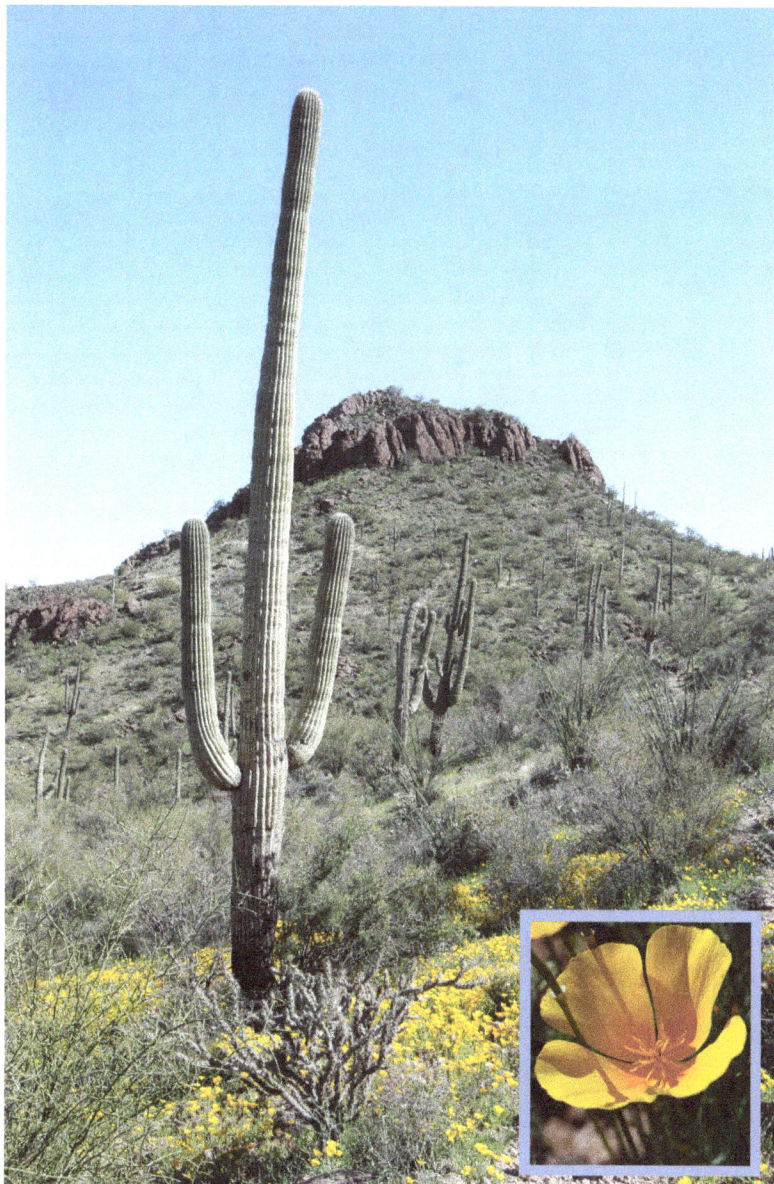

Characteristics of Complex Systems

"The intuitively obvious 'solutions' to social problems are apt to
fall into one of several traps set by the character of complex systems."

Jay W. Forrester, *World Dynamics*

Complex systems do not always act the way that people intuit. One way to understand the behaviors of these systems is to view them through a lens of common characteristics. Jay Forrester, MIT professor, developed and described these characteristics, given many years of exploring and modeling a variety of complex systems. His statement summarizes the importance of understanding these characteristics when working to address difficult social issues.

What are the characteristics of complex systems? Forrester described seven distinct characteristics (listed here along with additional explanations). The simulations, along with their accompanying materials, most closely demonstrate characteristic #4, although additional characteristics are also strongly embedded in some of the contexts.

Characteristics of Complex Systems

1. Cause and effect are not closely related in time or space.

Complex systems are composed of many interacting feedback loops. They often contain long time delays. What may appear to be an obvious reason for a particular problem is often not the fundamental cause of the problem, but only a symptom.

2. Action is often ineffective due to application of low-leverage policies.

Complex systems contain balancing feedback loops that surround the various goals of the system. Low-leverage policies often seem to be the "obvious" solutions to the problem at hand, but they encounter resistance – the tendency for interventions to be defeated by the response of the system to the intervention. Low-leverage policies are unable to overpower the balancing loops in order to align the competing goals of the system. In this complex system, the symptoms are commonly treated, rather than the problem.

3. High-leverage policies are difficult to apply correctly.

Complex systems contain areas of high leverage – places where a small push in the correct direction is likely to effect the desired change. In many cases, these high-leverage policies are difficult to identify and difficult to apply correctly. The "levers" for such policies may be pushed in the wrong direction, or not pushed at all.

4. The cause of the problem is within the system.

Problems observed in complex systems are almost always internally generated. While it is easier and more comfortable to place blame on others, it is more productive to look within the system itself to understand and change undesirable behavior. This complex system characteristic is often identified by the oscillation of the system.

---

5. Collapsing goals results in a downward spiral.

Complex systems tend to drift to lower levels of performance over time. This can occur over a long time-frame, making the downward spiral both insidious and hard to combat. This situation occurs when individuals or institutions respond to failing to reach their goals by adjusting them downward in order to relieve the discomfort of failure.

6. Conflicts arise between short-term and long-term goals.

In complex systems, there are tradeoffs between short-term and long-term goals. What is achievable or desirable within a short time-frame can reveal problematic consequences in the fullness of time. Conversely, concentrating on a future payoff almost always involves sacrifice in the present.

7. Burdens are shifted to the intervener.

This characteristic is often closely related to the tradeoff between short-term and long-term goals. Both play out over time, but the presence of an intervener usually means that a form of addiction or dependence is at work. The system's natural ability to fend for itself declines over time as the addiction/dependence becomes stronger.

Appendix B
System Dynamics Visual Tools

Behavior-over-time Graph

The variable being measured is always on the y-axis of the graph. Time is displayed on the x-axis. Depending on the context, the time frame could be short (measured in seconds) or long (measured in years). Most of the models in this series produce a variety of oscillatory behaviors, although other trends are also possible.

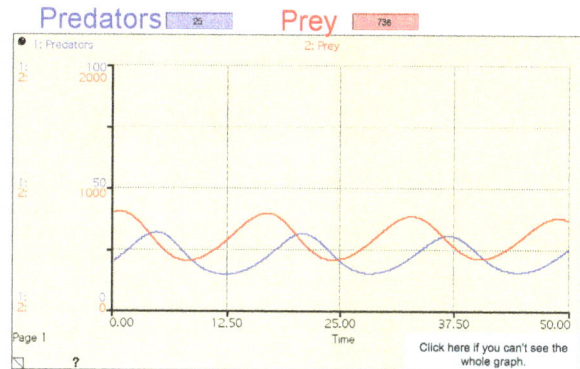

Causal Loop Diagram

A causal (or feedback) loop diagram is another visual tool that shows the structure of a system. A feedback loop tells a story about how a system operates. Any given system may have multiple interconnected loops. Arrows between any two elements indicate a cause-and-effect relationship: If the first element rises, then it causes the second element either to rise or fall. Depending on the relationship, different symbols are used. See the loop below along with the key explaining the different symbols.

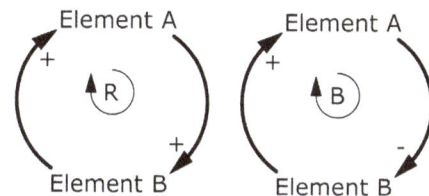

+   indicates a direct or additive relationship between the two elements.

-   indicates an indirect or subtractive relationship between the two elements.

R   in the middle indicates that the loop reinforces.

B   in the middle indicates that the loop balances.

Stock/Flow Map

A stock/flow map represents the structure of the system. The parts of the map along with the underlying mathematical assumptions define the nature of the interdependent relationships among the parts. This structure is based on assumptions about how the system (whether it be a spring or relationships on the playground) really works.

In its simplest form, a stock represents an accumulated amount and the flow (or flows) represent the rate at which the stock goes up or down. Other elements impact one or more flows, either adding to or subtracting from a stock.

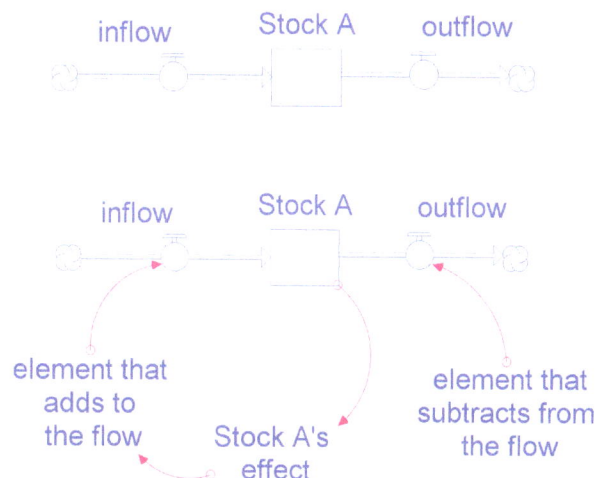

Appendix C
Technical Matters

Setting Up the Simulation

Menu System

Each simulation level has a standardized menu system displayed in a recommended order of use. Handouts guide students through all sections of each level's menu system.

Level A Menu

Level B Menu

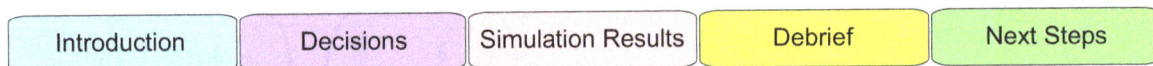

Level C Menu Example

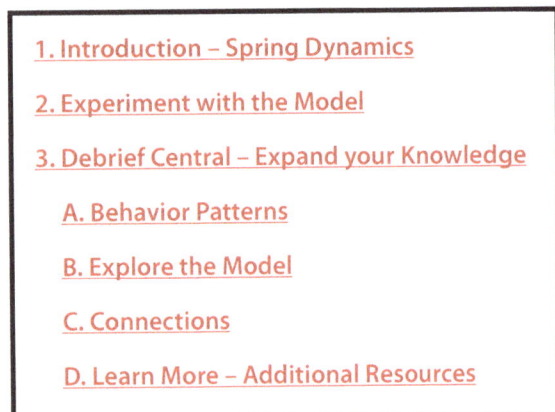

Home

Every screen has a "Home" button available. This button returns the user to the beginning title screen of the simulation.

Slidebars

Slidebars are one method for manipulating the settings for a simulation. Some of the slidebars have a general range, with no values showing. One example within the Level A – Spring Simulation shows a range of springiness from "easy to pull" to "hard to pull." Other simulations have slidebars that include numerical settings. The lesson handouts might ask the student to set a slidebar to a particular number.

General Range Slidebar

Move the Spring

very stretched · no push or pull · pushed up

Specific Numerical Slidebar

Initial position

Additional aspects of slidebars include:

- Setting a slidebar is as simple as moving the lever to the right or left to select higher or lower settings.
- Slidebars that have visible numerical values can also be set by clicking on the value in the middle and typing in the desired number.
- Slidebars must be set according the indicated minimum and maximum values. For example, if a range is 0–2000, the user will not be able to type in a value that exceeds 2000.
- Slidebars must be set by certain increments, depending on the variable. For example, if a range is 0–2000, then the increments may go up or down by increments of 100.

Knobs

Some of the Level C simulations contain one or more knobs on the control panel screen. These have minimum and maximum values and are set by moving the black dot around to the desired setting.

Buttons

Buttons are used throughout a simulation for different purposes, including navigation among the pages of the simulation, initiating a new simulation run, and resetting the simulation graphs. Depending on the level of the simulation, these buttons may be rectangular images or resemble links on a webpage.

Graphs

Graphs show simulation results as a behavior-over-time graph. The simulation lesson handouts for the B and C levels presume that students know how to create, title, label, and create a key for a line graph.

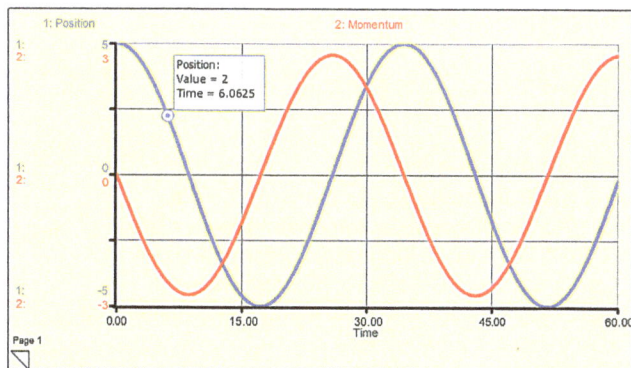

Some graphs may have multiple pages. To see the additional graphs, click on the tab ◿ at the bottom, left of the graph pad. Each time you click, the next graph appears. After clicking through all the graphs, the first one will again appear.

To see the actual values at any point on a graph line, click and hold the mouse arrow, right on the line at the point you'd like to check. A box will appear showing the value at a particular point in time.

Troubleshooting

"The simulation gives me a 'time out' message."

When running the simulation online, you may occasionally experience a "time out" message. This can occur for a variety of reasons, but the most common is when nothing on the simulation screen has been clicked for a while. If this happens, simply reload the page and return to the screen you last visited.

"The text and the graphics are all 'mixed up.'"

Occasionally, the development team updates simulations to improve them. If your computer browser has an old version saved in its memory, this can cause the simulation to display erroneous information. To fix this issue, you need to clear the cache from your browser. Browsers (e.g., Internet Explorer, Firefox, Safari) have different procedures for doing this, so see the help documentation for your browser if needed.

"The simulation behavior doesn't make sense."

Each of the simulation models in this series has limitations and is valid only when used within those limitations. If settings that exceed the model parameters are put into the simulation, the user may experience behavior on the graph that doesn't make sense.

For example, the animal population simulation shows the population trends for the animals included on the handouts. If the user tries to input data for an animal that has a very long lifespan and that frequently has many offspring, an exponential growth pattern may be produced. In reality, something else would limit the population growth, but the parameters of the simulation are not able to handle that extreme scenario.

See the accompanying background documents for additional information about the limitations of each model.

"I can't see the entire line on the graph."

In some cases, you may input settings that cause the behavior to go beyond the scale of a particular graph. If this occurs, most of the simulations have a button that allows the user to see the full graph. Note that no scale is set for this special graph, but rather a new scale (on the y-axis) is created with each new run.

"The QR codes are not working."

You can access all the simulations here:
https://exchange.iseesystems.com/profile/25/52

Background documents based on Level C simulations are available here:
Springs- http://static.clexchange.org/ftp/documents/x-curricular/CC2012_Oscillations1BackgroundInformation.pdf
Playground- http://static.clexchange.org/ftp/documents/x-curricular/CC2012_Oscillations2BackgroundInformation.pdf
Population- http://static.clexchange.org/ftp/documents/x-curricular/CC2012_Oscillations3BackgroundInformation.pdf
Pred/prey- http://static.clexchange.org/ftp/documents/x-curricular/CC2012_Oscillations4BackgroundInformation.pdf
Pred/prey/food- http://static.clexchange.org/ftp/documents/x-curricular/CC2012_Oscillations5_BackgroundInformation.pdf

About Us

About the Authors

Jennifer Andersen is a system dynamics professional who collaborates with the Creative Learning Exchange to create simulations for a wide audience. Since completing her education in simulation modeling fifteen years ago, she has consulted for many projects in the US, Scandinavia, Europe, and South America. She is particularly interested in promoting system dynamics as a tool for understanding complex systems and enhancing formal education in the STEM (Science, Technology, Engineering and Math) disciplines.

Anne LaVigne works with the Creative Learning Exchange and the Waters Foundation. She is a teacher, coach, instructional designer, and most importantly, a learner. For more than twenty years, she has collaborated with educators and students across K-12 settings using systems thinking and system dynamics tools. She strives to develop and share strategies for understanding dynamic, interdependent systems in ways that empower, engage, and motivate.

Lees Stuntz has worked for over twenty years encouraging the use of system dynamics and systems thinking in K-12 education. As Executive Director of the Creative Learning Exchange, she has created and edited multiple pieces of curriculum – available on the Creative Learning Exchange's website (www.clexchange.org), including seven books, as well as numerous curricular units. She collaborates with educators, system dynamicists and citizen advocates toward a collective goal of educating students to be effective systems citizens in our complex world.

The Creative Learning Exchange

The Creative Learning Exchange was founded as a non-profit organization in 1991 to encourage an active, learner-centered process of discovery for 5–19 year-old students that engages in meaningful, real-world problem solving through the mastery of systems thinking and system dynamics modeling. Since its inception, the CLE has worked to encourage teachers and educators to use systems thinking and system dynamics in classrooms and schools throughout the United States, as well as internationally. The CLE has done this through its website that offers free curriculum, its products that include books and games that promote systems thinking, and a biennial conference to help educators and students learn and utilize systems thinking and system dynamics in the classroom and the school organization.

System Dynamics and Jay Forrester

System dynamics is a field of study and a perspective for understanding change. Using computer simulation and other tools, system dynamics looks at how the feedback structure of systems causes the change we observe all around us. System dynamics was developed over fifty years ago by Professor Jay W. Forrester, MIT Professor Emeritus, and is used to address problems in areas ranging from ecology to business management, economics, and psychology. Under Forrester's guidance, system dynamics is helping teachers make K-12 education more learner-centered, engaging, challenging, and relevant to our rapidly changing world.

For more than twenty-five years, Professor Forrester has fostered this work within K-12 education. His direct support allowed the creation of these simulations and accompanying materials, which enables students to explore what are often befuddling characteristics of complex systems.

Led by a partnership between Dr. Forrester and the Creative Learning Exchange, the goal of this ongoing project is to create online curriculum materials for students, aged five and above, to illustrate characteristics of complex systems. In exploring the nature of complex social systems, the materials address questions such as:

- Why do such systems resist policy changes?
- Why are short-term and long-term responses to corrective action often at odds with each other?
- How can leverage points be applied to bring about desirable change in social systems?

The goals of the project are grounded in the belief that an abstract level of understanding of social systems will help prepare future citizens to actively shape their society.

www.ingramcontent.com/pod-product-compliance
Lightning Source LLC
Chambersburg PA
CBHW081300040426
42452CB00014B/2580